MW01714693

Roderic O'Conor / Vision and Expression

Roderic O'Conor

Vision and Expression

Hugh Lane
Municipal Gallery
of Modern Art

Dublin

Dr. Roy Johnston

This catalogue was published by the

Hugh Lane Municipal Gallery of Modern Art

Charlemont House
Parnell Square North
Dublin 1
Ireland
Tel: 353 1 874 1903
Fax: 353 1 872 2182
E-mail: HUGHLANE@iol.ie

The Gallery is funded by Dublin Corporation

British Library Cataloguing in Publication Data available.

ISBN 0 9514246 7 X

Edited by Christina Kennedy and Daire O'Connell
Photography by John Kellett
Designed and Produced by Creative Inputs
Colour Reproduction and Printing by Nicholson & Bass

Cover: *The Foaming Sea*, (detail) (cat. no. 4)

Contents

Author's Acknowledgments

I would like to acknowledge the help and encouragement of numerous collectors, curators, librarians and relatives of Roderic O'Conor who have helped me over the years in my research into his life and work. My work could not have been completed without their willingness to make their collections and archives available to me, and to answer my many questions.

In preparing for this exhibition of Roderic O'Conor's work I owe a special debt of thanks to Barbara Dawson, Director of the Hugh Lane Municipal Gallery of Modern Art, and to her patient and hard working staff, Christina Kennedy, Exhibitions Curator and Daire O'Connell. It has been a pleasure for me to work with all of them. Madame Catherine Puget, Conservateur du Musée de Pont-Aven in France has continued to be a supporter over the years, and I am grateful to her on this occasion for making available archival photographs of Pont-Aven for inclusion in the catalogue.

Finally this venture could not have been realised without the agreement of the several owners who have made their O'Conor paintings available to the Hugh Lane Gallery. I very much appreciate their support of my research over many years previous to this, and I am once again extremely grateful to them on this occasion.

Dr. Roy Johnston.

Foreword

Roderic O'Conor is a unique figure in the context of Irish art. His early training was typical for the period; he studied at the Metropolitan School of Art in Dublin and exhibited at the Royal Hibernian Academy annual exhibitions before moving to Antwerp where he studied at Academie Royale des Beaux Arts between 1883 and 1884. When he arrived in Paris in 1886, unlike his fellow Irish artists, O'Conor, abandoning his formal academic training, rapidly moved to the fore of the avant garde. His stylish experimentation was further encouraged when he moved to Brittany in 1891. There he became part of the Pont-Aven School, a loosely formed group of artists who were drawn together by Paul Gauguin's theories on Synthetism in art which echoed Symbolist thinking in literature. The group advocated a re-evaluation of aesthetic ideals favouring a more subjective response to nature. In 1956 when the critic Clive Bell saw O'Conor's work from this period he commented "*These pictures painted at the beginning of the century are sometimes oddly like what daring young men were to paint ten years later.*"

Previously a neglected figure in the history of modern art Roderic O'Conor's contribution to painting is gradually being re-assessed. Our Roderic O'Conor room contains significant examples of the artist's work from 1886 to c.1920. The room celebrates his gift of *Une Jeune Bretonne* to the collection in 1904, the first O'Conor painting to enter a public collection. The paintings in this room reveal the artist's innovation and remarkable talent.

The O'Conor room could not have happened without the willing consent of the lenders to whom we are extremely grateful.The publication of the catalogue was generously sponsored by Larry Powell and Mervyn Solomon. Dr. Roy Johnston's work on O'Conor has been largely responsible for a renewed interest in the artist and this catalogue which examines in detail O'Conor's early years in France is a valuable addition to the documentation of this period.

Barbara Dawson,
Director.

Self Portrait, *1903?*
Oil on canvas
54.6 x 45.7 cms
Courtesy, National Gallery of Ireland
(not in exhibition)

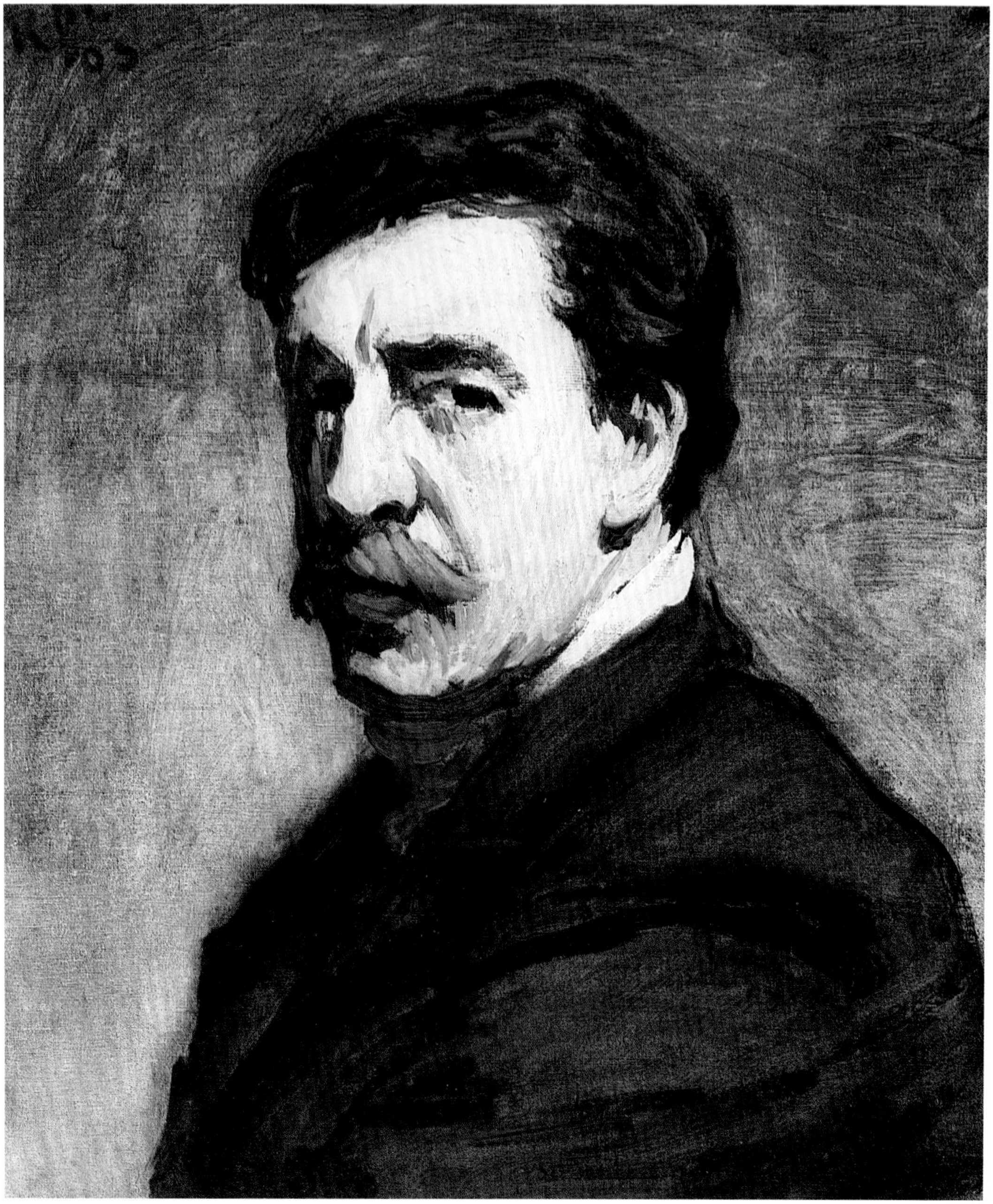

Introduction

Roderic Anthony O'Conor 1860-1940

Roderic Anthony O'Conor was born in County Roscommon in 1860 and he died in France in 1940, having spent all of his mature years as an artist outside his native Ireland.

In the course of the last fifteen years, O'Conor's life and work has been the subject of several published articles, a couple of television documentaries, two retrospective exhibitions, a doctoral dissertation and a book. [1] Although the research has been extensive, many of his paintings still remain untraced and there are periods in his life which still have to yield useful information about his work habits, and his art. As each new painting of quality comes on the market however, that early impression of him as being one of Ireland's most distinguished artists is further confirmed.

It is true that not all of O'Conor's work is of consistently high quality, but then that can be said of almost every artist. The circumstances of O'Conor's death in 1940, the subsequent harbouring of his paintings by his widow until her death in 1955, and their eventual release through the well documented studio sale at Hôtel Drouot in Paris in 1956, was not a process which maintained any control over the quality of paintings which passed into the hands of private buyers and dealers. Some of the paintings were unfinished, many had no titles and were not signed, and some were his wife's rather than his.

The being said, O'Conor's best work is outstanding and wholly pertinent to its time. When considered in the context of the period in which they were created, and this is especially true of his Brittany pictures between 1892-1895, his paintings stand as the most progressive work ever produced by an Irish artist.

To be an O'Conor from Connaught is to be a member of one of Ireland's most distinguished families. Indeed, few families can claim to have made as great a contribution to the development of Ireland's social, political and economic cultural past as the Roscommon O'Conors. Roderic O'Conor could trace his ancestry back to the last Kings of Ireland, although he made little mention of this in the artistic circles in which he moved in France.

He was born at Milltown, between Tulsk and Castleplunkett, as the second eldest child in an eventual family of six. His father was in the legal profession and became High Sheriff of County Roscommon, and his mother Eleanor Mary Browne was from a well known land owning family in County Meath. The family home, Milltown House, was at the end of a tree lined avenue half a mile long, past a gate lodge, and was surrounded by 640 acres of farm land.

Coming from such a background, an education in England was inevitable and when he was thirteen O'Conor was sent to the Benedictines at Ampleforth College in Yorkshire. After his English education ended in 1878, he shunned the idea of entering one of the professions and chose instead to study art at the Metropolitan School in Dublin. In 1883 he moved on to the Académie des Beaux-Arts in Antwerp to further his studies there, stayed for only one year and returned to Dublin where he exhibited at the Royal Hibernian Academy in 1885.

In common with so many other young international artists of his generation, O'Conor found the attractions and artistic energy of Paris to be irresistible. He left Dublin for Paris in 1886, studied initially with the portrait painter Carolus Duran and had his work accepted at the official Salon in 1888 and again in 1889. Simultaneously, he was experimenting with Impressionist techniques, working in the landscape around Grez-sur-Loing to the South of Fontainebleau, and his work quickly departed from its academic origins to absorb all that was then new in French painting.

O'Conor moved to Brittany and Pont-Aven in 1891 and was accepted as a member of the group which had formed around Paul Gauguin a couple of years earlier, in response to his new approach to painting embracing the ideals embodied in the Symbolist movement of the time. He painted vigorous landscapes in a style derived from Van Gogh, shared in the group's discussions without making a total commitment to their ideas, and painted bold and expressive paintings in his own distinctively striped style.

The Village of Pont-Aven, Brittany

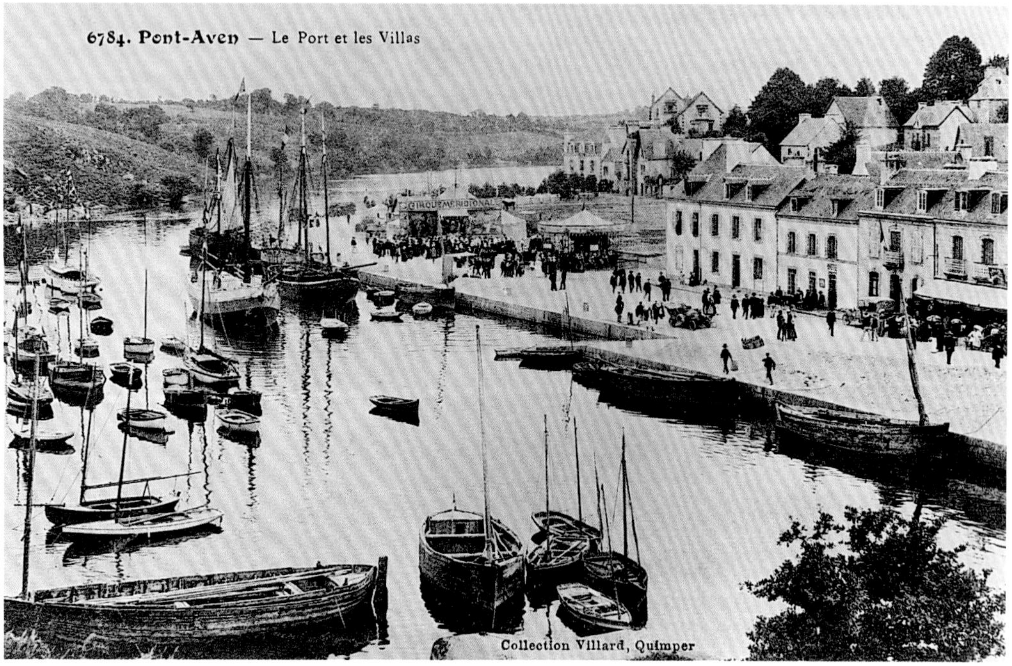

When Gauguin's group began to break up and go their separate ways following their leader's final departure for the South Seas, O'Conor withdrew for several years to Rochefort-en-Terre in Morbihan. After a brief visit to Pont-Aven he returned to Paris shortly after the death of his closest friend Armand Seguin late in 1903. He took a studio in Montparnasse in 1904 which became his base for the next thirty years, and there he painted the traditional subjects of the studio artist - still life pictures, portraits, figures in interiors, and many sensuous nudes. When he wanted access to landscape themes he made the short journey from Paris to Grez-sur-Loing. He also visited Cassis in the South of France where he painted in the summer of 1913 and he travelled to the museums of Italy and Spain when he wanted to study the old masters whom he much admired.

O'Conor's paintings in Paris showed little influence from any of the great twentieth century movements which were developing around him. As the century unfolded his work reflected something of Renoir whom he much admired, and then of Bonnard whose "Intimisme" and sensitive colour range seemed to inspire him. He remained faithful to his basic philosophy as an artist who always preferred to work from things seen and observed, painting after 1915 in a style best described as expressive realism.

Late in his life, O'Conor married a much younger woman, Renée Honta, who was initially his model, and then his mistress before they were married in 1933. They bought a house in the West of France at Nueil-sur-Layon in Maine-et-Loire, where he died in 1940, and there his body rests in the local cemetery.

1. Publications on Roderic O'Conor, which collectively give a complete account of his life and work, are listed in the bibliography.

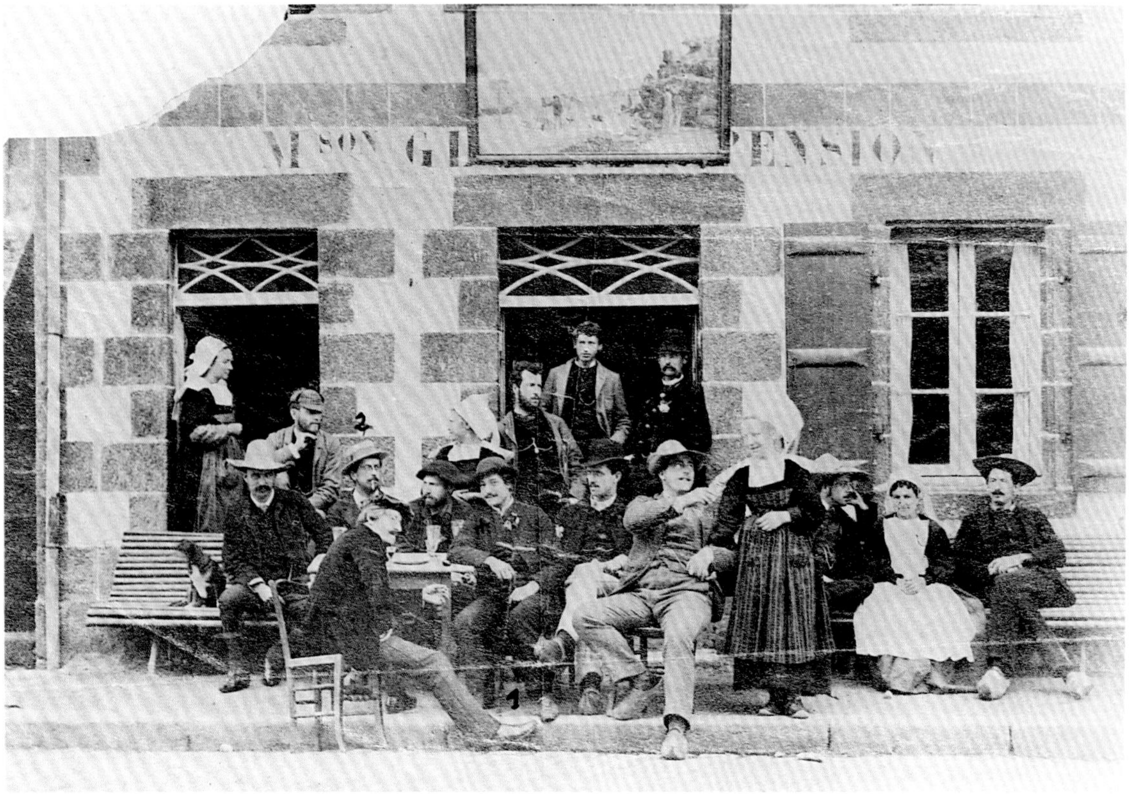

A group of painters and local residents outside the Pension Gloanec in Pont-Aven.

Roderic O'Conor

Exhibitions and the Critics

The recognition of Roderic O'Conor's considerable gifts as a painter is by no means a recent phenomenon. His reputation had already been made in Paris during the last decade of the nineteenth century, and there is ample supporting evidence of his unquestionable talent from artists and critics who were then familiar with his work.

Of the many myths about O'Conor, one which has been slow to dispel is the belief that he studiously avoided exhibiting his work during his career. He certainly had no enthusiasm for any affiliation with the Parisian commercial galleries, and despite his absence from all exhibitions of any type there between 1894 and 1902, the facts are that outside these dates he showed on an almost annual basis in forty five salon exhibitions between 1888 and 1935.[1] In this period approximately two hundred paintings were exhibited, many of which still remain untraced.

O'Conor arrived in France in 1886 and made his first appearance in a Paris exhibition two years later at the official Salon. His portrait of the Danish artist Paul Vogelius was influenced by Carolus Duran, a fashionable society painter in whose atelier he was then studying. He exhibited again at the Salon in 1889 and later in the same year he showed three paintings at the much more progressive Salon des Indépendants, in an exhibition in which the then unknown van Gogh was represented by two works. O'Conor's appearance in two such contrasting exhibitions in the same year confirms that his painting style was undergoing an early process of change and transformation.

A brief but important clue to the appearance of O'Conor's 1889 pictures was provided by the critic Martel Toussaint, in his review of the Salon des Indépendants exhibition.[2] After considering the Pointillist or Neo-Impressionist works exhibited by Cross, Signac, Luce and Pissarro, Toussaint referred to 'les flamboyants paysages de M. O'Conor'. His use of a descriptive adjective meaning 'blazing' or 'fiery', confirms that O'Conor was then already committed to the use of a rich and colourful palette. In 1890 O'Conor returned to the Indépendants with ten paintings, the same number as van Gogh, and in 1892 his first paintings with Breton titles were exhibited.

Brittany, and in particular the small town of Pont-Aven which had been an artists' colony since at least 1866, had the greatest possible significance for O'Conor. When he arrived there in 1891, he was quickly accepted into membership of the international group of artists, later to become known as the School of Pont-Aven, which had formed around Paul Gauguin in 1888 in response to his new ideas about symbolism and syntheticism in painting. The young Swiss painter Cuno Amiet, then in Pont-Aven, described O'Conor to his sister as 'a painter with a significant talent whose name during the last year has started becoming well known in Paris'.[3] We also know from Amiet that

O'Conor sold a painting in the 1892 Indépendants and in the same letter to his father he wrote 'I think with the works he has on exhibition this year (1893) he will be extraordinarily successful'.[4]

The dominant influence in O'Conor's Brittany paintings between 1892 and 1895 is clearly from Van Gogh, but in his use of rhythmic lines and decorative contours, flattening of pictorial space, and non-naturalistic and intense colour range, he also acknowledges a debt to Gauguin's version of Syntheticism which was at the core of his new approach to painting.

When the avant-garde symbolist writer Alfred Jarry met O'Conor in Pont-Aven in 1894, he was aware of some scepticism on the Irishman's part about the group's ideas. Jarry later published an article on the painter Filiger in *Mercure de France*, in which he commented on the choice of subject matter made by the artist to express 'beauty', and he drew this conclusion: 'in his (O'Conor's) case there is a slight disdain towards making a choice at all, his belief being that the painter is outside time and therefore not concerned with place or space either'.[5] Taking her cue from the evidence of Jarry's dialogue with O'Conor, Jaworska, in the first comprehensive study of the School of Pont-Aven concluded: 'he (O'Conor) painted in a state of perpetual revolt against all considerations of theory', adding that he stopped short of fully embracing Gauguin's ideas.[6]

O'Conor's well documented friendship with Gauguin can be dated to 1894, the year Gauguin returned to Pont-Aven after his first visit to Tahiti. Equally well documented is the fact that Gauguin thought O'Conor was about to accompany him on what was to prove to be his final journey to the South Seas in 1895.[7] As we now know O'Conor did not go, and we can only speculate on what the outcome for his work, and indeed for Irish painting would have been, had he travelled with Gauguin.

Clive Bell, whom O'Conor was to meet some ten years later in Paris when he was a young graduate student, described this friendship as 'the great event in O'Conor's life' and added: 'what to me seems clear is that Gauguin's strength of character and convincing style of talk made a deep impression on the young, or youngish Irishman.'[8]

The annual Salon exhibitions were large and confusing affairs, and O'Conor enjoyed a much better platform for his paintings at this period in his career, in smaller and more select group shows in Paris. At Le Barc de Boutteville's gallery at 47 rue Peletier in Montmartre, described by one writer as 'the true birthplace of modern painting', [9] he showed on three occasions in 1894, and once in 1895, in the company of Bonnard, Gauguin, Guillaumin, Lautrec, Loiseau, and Sérusier. Group exhibitions there were shown under the general title 'Peintres Impressionnistes et Symbolistes', a title which Le Barc had borrowed from the café Volpini exhibition of 1889, where Gauguin and his followers had exhibited their new work for the first time.

Once again one of the Parisian writers, this time the highly respected critic Léon-Paul Fargue

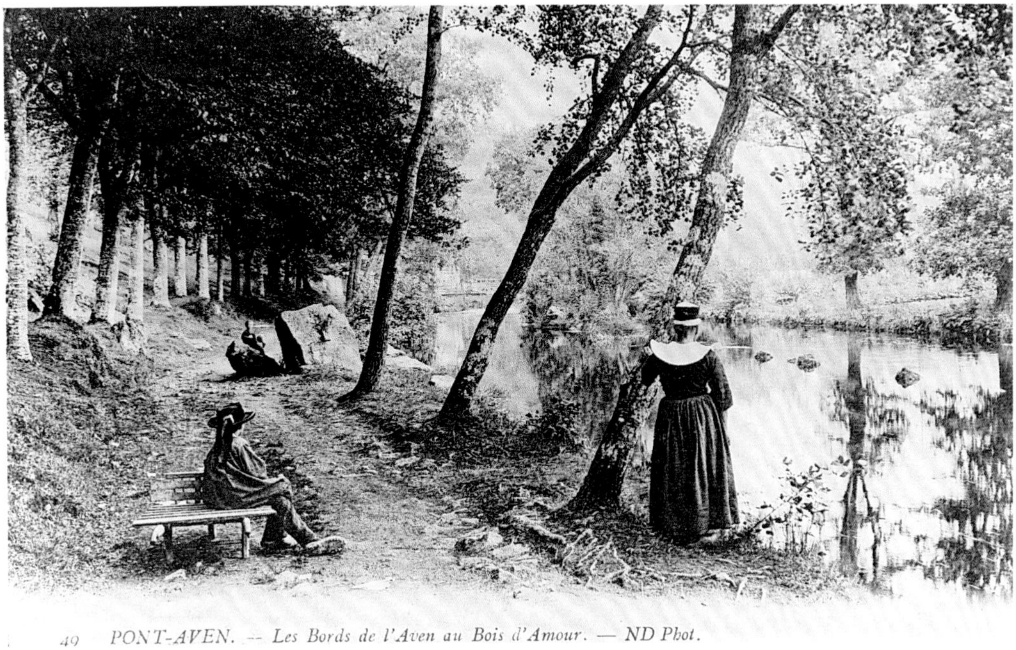

Pont-Aven.
The banks of the river Aven.

identified with O'Conor's work, and wrote to him in connection with an article which he was then in the course of preparing.[10] Fargue was commissioned to write a type of artistic profile on O'Conor for the second volume in the series '*Portraits du prochaine siècle - poètes et prosateurs*', published by the review '*Essais d'Art Libre*', which was to include notes on selected painters, sculptors, and printmakers. O'Conor's name was included with others in the pre-publicity, but unfortunately the second volume was never printed. A published article devoted to O'Conor at that time (in 1894) when he was clearly at the peak of his creative powers, would have had the highest possible significance for him, and would certainly have consolidated his reputation in Parisian art circles.

When O'Conor exhibited in the same gallery in July of 1894, his four paintings, each entitled 'Paysage', merited a passing reference in the Parisian review *l'Ymagier*. Later the critic René Barjean writing in Essais d'Art Libre, made this reference to O'Conor's exhibits: '...deux paysages, signés O'Connor (sic). Quel chantre émis de la lumière! Il ne semble pas qu'on ait jusqu'ici proclamé suffisamment l'atelier rayonnement de ses hymnes.'[11] Once again it was O'Conor's distinctive use of light and colour which drew the critical praise.

Before the end of the century there was further recognition of O'Conor's artistic status, this time from outside Fance. He received an invitation to exhibit with the avant-garde group in Belgium who were known as 'La Libre Esthétique'.[12] He showed with this group in Brussels in 1898, and again in 1905, along with Maurice Denis, James Ensor, Aristide Maillol, the Neo-Impressionist Théo van Rysselberghe, and others.

There were mixed responses from the critics reviewing the 1898 exhibition. One wrote in praise of an O'Conor landscape painting, describing it as being 'filled with beautiful light' while also commenting on the warm colours of his painting of flowers. Another critic described his colour as being 'garish'.

In 1905 the art critic of '*Le Soir*' commented that the invited foreign section only offered a few works of real interest but chose to specifically mention O'Conor's painting of a 'tumultuous wave'.[13] In '*Le Petit Messager Belge*', in reference to two paintings of fruit and of crockery, the critic commented that he was perhaps the painter who knew best how to render the material which he wished to represent.

When the Salon d'Automne opened its doors to a new generation of artists in 1903, O'Conor was one of its first exhibitors, and he sustained a long commitment to this annual exhibition as a sociétaire, missing only two shows in subsequent years up to 1935.

O'Conor's work in the first Salon d'Automne attracted the attention of the Paris dealer Clovis Sagot who was already an advocate of a new tendency in painting which was to emerge in 1905 as Fauvism. Sagot wrote to O'Conor offering to represent him, but true to form O'Conor did not take up the offer.[14] If he had done so, it would surely have been of the greatest possible significance for him, as Sagot was to exhibit Georges Braque's early fauvist works in the following year.

O'Conor's earlier friendship with Gauguin had given him a unique status in Parisian art circles. Included in the 1906 Salon d'Automne was a large tribute exhibition to Gauguin consisting of 227 examples of his work. The critic Charles Morice, in the introduction to the catalogue, acknowledged O'Conor both as a lender and as a confidante of Gauguin's. Morice also wrote separately of O'Conor in the *Mercure de France*:

> 'O'Conor, who is closer to Gauguin in feeling and vision, but less didactic, less inclined to base himself on a doctrine whose inventor professed it whenever he was not painting but took liberties with it in order to paint masterpieces - O'Conor recalls him to our memories, with an accent of emotion and tenderness which indicates a personal nature and gives promise of future discoveries.'[15]

O'Conor also appeared in the 1906 exhibition in profile view in a large work by Paul Girieud painted as an act of homage to Gauguin's memory. The setting for Girieud's painting was a rather arid landscape sparsely dotted with trees, in which a number of Gauguin's friends join the master for an exotic feast in a composition which recalls Leonardo's 'The Last Supper'.[16]

O'Conor did not exhibit in the 1907 Salon d'Automne as he was on the selection jury reviewing paintings by artists of the status of Bonnard, Braque, Dufy, Matisse, Modigliani, Rouault and Sickert. In spite of his general dissatisfaction with the jury process which he conveyed to Clive Bell,[17] he also served as vice-president of the jury two years later with Charles Plumet, assisting in the selection of the 1909 exhibition which included Brancusi, Duchamp, Kandinsky, John Lavery, and Vlaminck.

These large salon exhibitions, which were eagerly looked forward to by the exhibition going public and the art critics of Paris, were frequently overhung and excessively crowded as so many artists looked to the Salons as the first level of exposure for the previous year's paintings. In 1907 there were 571 artists exhibiting 1,748 works at the Salon d'Automne, and in 1908 at the Salon des Indépendants the totals were a staggering 1,314 artists exhibiting no fewer than 6,701 works. O'Conor made a reference to the scale of the exhibition in a letter sent to Clive Bell in 1908 when he wrote: 'The Indépendants open the middle of next month. I am sending 5 or 6 things, but in such a rout of bad and muddling things do not expect to be seen. It is the only place I approve of however.'[18]

In spite of the immense scale of these exhibitions, O'Conor's painting 'Repos' caught the eye of the wealthy Russian collector Ivan Morosov who purchased it from the 1905 Salon des Indépendants. Morosov had been buying the work of modern French painters since 1903, and his collection included works by Cezanne, van Gogh, Gauguin, Monet, Renoir and Sisley. Through the Morosov connection, O'Conor's painting now hangs in the collection of the Hermitage Museum in Leningrad.

In 1913 several of O'Conor's exhibits at the Salon d'Automne were from Cassis in the south of France, where he had been painting that summer, and once again a distinguished critic linked him and his work to Gauguin. This time it was Guillaume Apollinaire who wrote: 'Salle XII....le mordant, bon peintre de la Bretagne O'Connor (sic) qui conserve avec un soin jaloux la tradition qu'il recut de Gauguin,'...[19]

Although O'Conor's career in the twentieth century evolved quite separately from the Fauvist, Cubist, Expressionist, and Surrealist movements, he continued to receive international invitations to exhibit. In 1904 Hugh Lane included O'Conor's touching painting of a young Breton girl in mourning (cat. no.11) in the exhibition of Irish painters shown at the Guildhall in London. He was also represented in the Trinational Exhibition of 1925 which was shown in Paris, London, and New York, and in the Carnegie International Exhibitions of 1924 and 1925. Roger Fry invited him to exhibit in 1928 at the Museo Nationale in Buenos Aires, where he showed two paintings in a major exhibition of British painting titled 'Aristas Britanicos'.[20]

Corporation of London Art Gallery Loan Collection of pictures of the Irish School, 1904 (organised by Hugh Lane)

8 CATALOGUE, LOAN COLLECTION, 1904.

23. UNE JEUNE BRETONNE.

By RODERICK O'CONOR. Canvas 36 × 29 inches. Lent by the Artist.

In the process of showing in such distinguished company it was natural that O'Conor should gain the respect of many of the artists who were then living in Paris and who have since become familiar names. In the 1920's, Bell discovered that in conversation Dunoyer de Segonzac, referred to the Irishman as "Père O'Conor".[21] Bell also recorded that when he was in Paris as a young man, O'Conor and his Canadian painter friend J.W. Morrice 'played as influential a part in my life as any of my Cambridge contemporaries'.[22] Bell added that O'Conor's paintings then looked like what younger artists were to paint ten years later.

O'Conor certainly held strong opinions about painting and art in general, and he could be extremely cynical in his condemnation of those whose work he did not like. However the most frustrating thing in any study of O'Conor, must surely be that outside of those opinions there is practically no evidence of any theoretical stance in any personal writing, or in any of his letters which have survived.

Why should this be? Why should it be the case that an artist who was well known for his forthright opinions on painting, and who was not afraid to express these to an eager audience of friends and confidantes, chose for the greater part of his career to remain outside of all contemporary theory? Despite his membership of Gauguin's circle, O'Conor in retrospect can be seen to have been a traditionalist at heart with an approach to painting in the twentieth century which never really escaped from its nineteenth century origins. Although a significant number of later paintings of real quality have emerged in recent years, they fit most easily into an approach to painting associated with that large grouping of emigré artists loosely defined as 'Ecole de Paris', rather than into any one of the twentieth century 'isms'.

We might speculate on why it was that O'Conor kept clear of the dealers, especially as he did buy and collect the work of other artists and he traded their work back into the same system, through some of the same dealers that he rejected for handling his own work.[23] Given what we know about his cynical attitude and heavy criticism of work which he considered inferior, he would have lost all credibility among his own circle of admirers if he had become an active participant in the same system of which he was so critical. The fact that he had an assured private income after his father's death in 1893, meant of course that he had no compelling need to sell his paintings to meet his everyday expenses.

However now that the years of recent research have given us a more comprehensive view of his life's work, it also becomes more clear that O'Conor did not always sustain a lasting commitment to themes or ideas in his painting as his career unfolded. Periods of relative inactivity seem to have contributed something to this lack of continuity and his eclecticism makes for difficulties in establishing a clear chronology for paintings as they have emerged. As every artist knows, a successful solo exhibition demands some degree of unity and coherence in a body of work if it is to have a chance of being critically accepted. In contrast the large salon exhibitions afforded him the opportunity to exhibit a small group of pictures in the comparative security of the group context.

Because almost all of O'Conor's activity as an artist was outside Ireland, he can claim no direct influence on the work of other Irish artists of his generation. His place in Irish art is however unique, precisely for the reason that his success was achieved outside Ireland in the critically demanding context of avant-garde painting in late nineteenth century France. With the benefit of hindsight we can place him close to the point of genesis of a significant historical development in art when he was in company with Paul Gauguin and his circle at Pont-Aven.

O'Conor's affiliation with these artists took place after their group had formed, at a time when their agenda was already established. Nevertheless he was welcomed as a valued member of their circle not just for his knowledge about painting in general, but more especially for the quality and contemporary relevance of his own painting. Such qualities did not escape the attention of the most influential and important critics of the period. When writers of the stature of Charles Morice, Guillaume Apollinaire, Alfred Jarry, and Léon-Paul Fargue singled his work out for critical attention, they also unwittingly afforded him special recognition as an artist who was not French, but who had completely assumed that identity in his own painting. For that reason alone he fully justifies his reputation as the most advanced Irish, or for that matter British artist of his generation.

1. O'Conor exhibited at the Salon des indépendants in 1889/90/92/93 and from 1903-1908. He showed at the Salon d'Automne from 1903-1906, and from 1908-32 without interruption, exhibiting finally with this group in 1934 and 1935. He also exhibited at the Salon des Tuileries from 1923-1930 with the exception of the year 1929. There were no salon exhibitions in Paris during the war years from 1914-1918.
2. The original article has been re-published in *Un Siècle d'Art Moderne, L'Histoire du Salon des Indépendants,* editions Denrel, (1984). See the chapter by André Parinaud, 'Les Indépendants,; la critique et la presse, l'affirmation de la Modernité 1884-1914,' p.94
3. Cuno Amiet to his sister, in a letter from Pont-Aven dated 21 December '92. Private collection, Switzerland.
4. Amiet to his father, letter dated 7 March'93. Private collection, Switzerland.
5. Jarry, Alfred, 'Filiger', *Mercure de France,* septembre 1894, pp 73-77
6. Jaworska, Wladyslawa, *Gauguin and the Pont-Aven School,* London 1972, p.221
7. Malingue, M. *Paul Gauguin lettres à sa femme et à ses amis,* Paris 1946. See the letter written by Gauguin in September of 1894 from Pont-Aven to his musician friend in Paris, William Molard, in which he relayed this information.
8. Bell, Clive, *Old Friends,* London (1956) p.166
9. Humbert, Agnes. *Les Nabis et leur Epoque,* 1888-1900, Genève (1954), p.95
10. Letter from Léon-Paul Fargue to Roderic O'Conor, April 30 1984. Private collection, France.
11. Barjean, René. *Essais d'Art Libre,* aout/septembre/octobre 1894, p.198
12. The group had originally been known as 'Les Vingt' or 'Les XX' when they formed an exhibiting group in 1883 as a more progressive alternative to the conservative policies of the Brussels Salon. Reorganised in 1893 as 'La Libre Esthétique', they had a policy of inviting notable Belgian and foreign artists to exhibit with them. For information about 'La Libre Esthétique' see Maus, Madeleine Octave, *Trente années de lutte pour l'art,* 1884-1914, Brussels 1926. In 1898 O'Conor was represented by five paintings and in 1904 he showed four works.
13. Exhibited as 'La Vague' (79), now in the collection of York City Art Gallery.
14. Letter from Clovis Sagot to Roderic O'Conor dated 20 November 1903, in which he commented favourably on O'Conor's work at the Salon d'Automne. Private collection, France.
15. Morice, Charles, 'Vingtième Salon des Indépendants', *Mercure de France*, April 1906
16. Girieud's painting entitled 'Hommage à Gauguin' also included Sérusier, Maurice Denis, Daniel de Monfried, Charles Morice and Girieud with others.
17. In a letter to Clive Bell sent from Paris on 18 February 1908 O'Conor wrote: 'Since I was on the jury of the Salon d'Automne last year I have nothing but disgust left for juries'. Collection of the National Gallery of Ireland.
18. ibid
19. Apollinaire, Guillaume, *l'Intransigeant*, 18 novembre 1913
20. Fry had been elected to a committee supported by Lord Duveen, which had been charged with the responsibility of promoting British art abroad. O'Conor's exhibits were 'La Bandera', No. 183 (£100) and 'Jardin en Cassis', No. 184 (£100). Others exhibiting with him included Vanessa Bell, Jacob Epstein, Duncan Grant, Augustus John, Paul Nash, Walter Sickert, Matthew Smith and Stanley Spencer.
21. Bell. op cit p. 169
22. ibid. p. 139
23. O'Conor had a refined eye and bought and sold paintings and collected the work of those artists he admired. In 1956 at the disposal of his collection there were 34 prints by Gauguin, 36 by Redon and 39 by Toulouse Lautrec. He owned work by his contemporaries Bernard, Fillger, Slewinski, and Seguin. He bought Bonnard, Cezanne, Goya, Manet, Munch, Pissarro, Renoir, Vuillard, Delacroix, Derain, Luce, Modigliani, and Vlaminck.

Catalogue

Works exhibited

1	*Groupe de peupliers,* 1886
2	*Landscape with road and farm buildings,*circa 1889
3	*La lisière du bois,* 1890
4	*The foaming sea,* 1892
5	*Head of a Breton boy,* circa 1893
6	*L'approche de Lezaven,* circa 1894
7	*Landscape,* circa 1897-'98
8	*Blue sea and rocks, Brittany,* circa 1898
9	*Paysage avec moutons,* circa 1900
10	*Personnages avec cheval,* circa 1900
11	*Une Jeune Bretonne,* 1903
12	*Boulevard Raspail,* circa 1905-'06
13	*Reclining female nude,* circa 1907-'09
14	*Nature morte,* 1909
15	*Bowl of roses,* circa 1914
16	*Nature morte - Fruits,* 1915
17	*La jeune fille,* circa 1920

List of abbreviations

Insc.	Inscription
Exh.	Exhibition record
Prov.	Provenance
Lit.	Literature
Ill.	Illustrated
s.t.l./t.r.	Signed top left/top right
d.t.l./t.r.	Dated top left/top right

oil on canvas
64.1 x 54.0 cms.
s.b.l.f. R. O'Conor
d.b.l.f. 1886

Prov: Given by Roderic O'Conor to Francis Chadwick at Grez-sur-Loing; by descent to Mme. Corrine Colombe; purchased by present owner 1983.

Exh: London, Belfast, Dublin, Manchester, *Roderic O'Conor 1860-1940*, 1985, (3) ill. p.18; Dublin, Hugh Lane Municipal Gallery of Modern Art, *Frank O'Meara and his contemporaries*, 1989 (22) ill.

Lit: Hill 1983, p.18; Benington 1985, p.253, ill. p.254 (as 'Autumn Landscape'); Benington 1992 (4)

Private collection

Groupe de peupliers

Group of poplars

This is the earliest known work which has been traced to date which reveals O'Conor's adoption of an Impressionist influenced style. He is believed to have arrived in Paris in 1886, co-incidentally in the same year as the last Impressionist group exhibition.

From the evidence of this painting, probably painted in the autumn of 1886, it appears that once in France he wasted little time in leaving the naturalism of his earlier landscapes for the more spontaneous approach of the Impressionists. There were many examples of their work to be seen in Paris and O'Conor's first introduction to their paintings could have been at Durand-Ruel's gallery, or at the Salon des Indépendants exhibition in August and September.

The location for the painting is probably Grez-sur-Loing to the south of Paris just outside Fontainebleau, where there was a lively colony of American, British, and Scandinavian artists centred on the Hotel Chevillion which overlooked an old bridge spanning the river. O'Conor's early involvement with the Impressionist's style rather set him apart from the rest of the Grez artists, most of whom were influenced by the work of Bastian-Lepage.

O'Conor exhibited a painting entitled 'Groupe de peupliers - effet de soleil' (188), at the 1889 Salon des Indépendants, although in the absence of any inscriptions by the artist on the reverse we cannot be certain that this is the same work. Many of O'Conor's paintings have been given their titles by successive owners and this work is also known as 'Autumn landscape'.

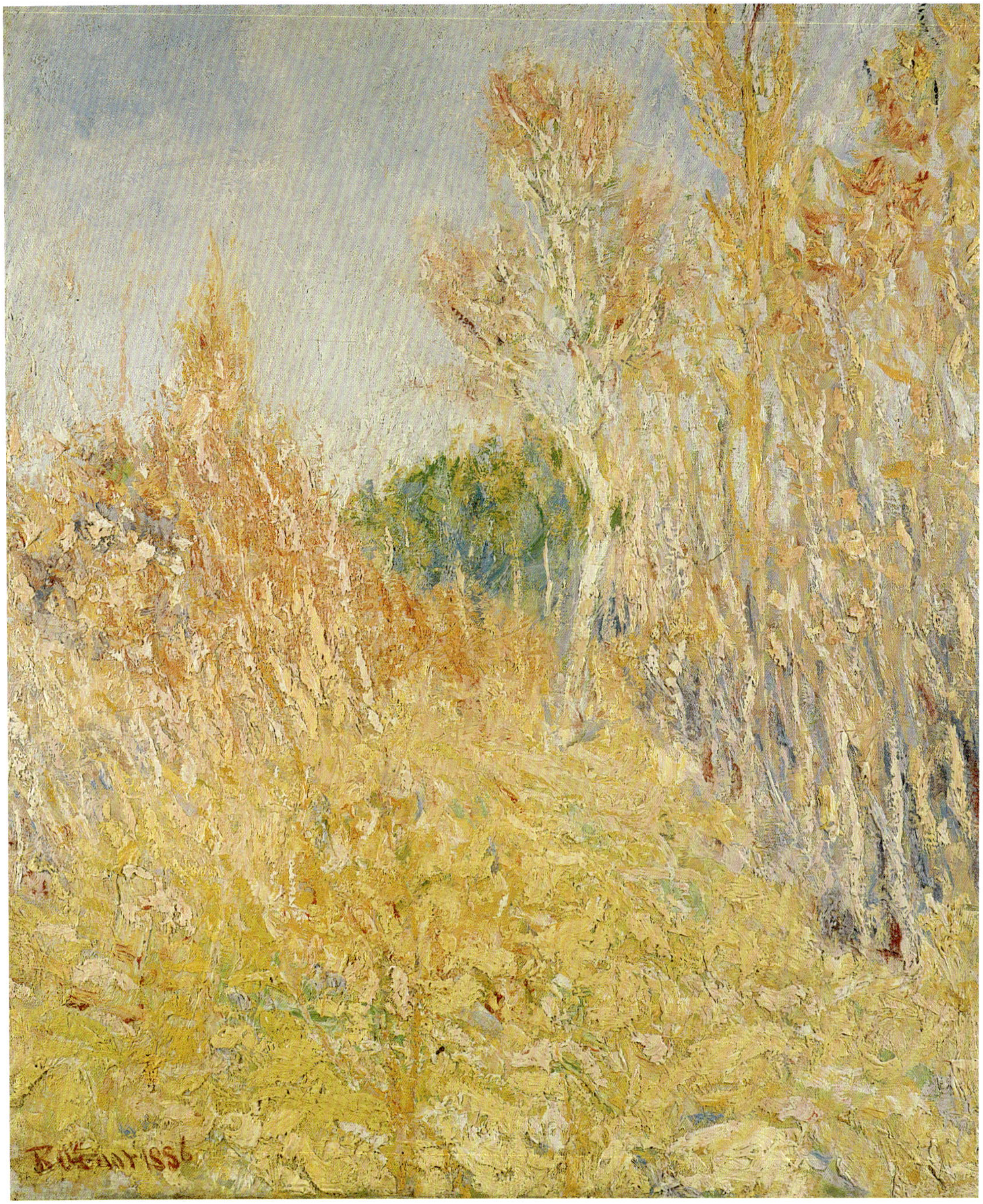

circa 1889
oil on canvas
54.6 x 64.7 cms.
s.b.r.f. R. O'Conor

Landscape with road and farm buildings

Prov: Godolphin Gallery, Dublin 1978; private collection.

Exh: Dublin 1978 Godolphin Gallery (ex cat.) ill; Pont-Aven, *Roderic O'Conor 1860-1940*, Musèe de Pont-Aven 1984 (2) ill. p.36; London, Belfast, Dublin, Manchester, *Roderic O'Conor 1860-1940*, 1985, (5) ill. p.63.

Lit: Lynch 1980, p.21 ill.; Benington 1992 (8).

Private collection

The features of the landscape in this painting also suggest the flat landscape typical of the environs of Grez-sur-Loing where O'Conor was in residence from 1889-90. Grez was easily reached from Paris by train to the nearby station at Montigny, and this as much as anything had contributed to its popularity with the numerous artists who painted there. Other Irish painters including Frank O'Meara, John Lavery and Katherine MacCausland had also worked at Grez, and there was an almost continual presence of international painters in residence in the village.

The painting is an excellent example of O'Conor's early incursion into Impressionist techniques with the forms of the landscape and the houses being captured economically, with a sense of directness and freshness in the painting. There is very little preliminary drawing in evidence, and the paint has been applied directly to the canvas with a technique which effectively combines brush and palette knife.

O'Conor exhibited a painting 'Chemin menant à Grez' in the 1890 Salon des Indépendants, and although it is tempting to link this painting to that exhibition, there are no inscriptions on the reverse to confirm that this work and the 1890 Salon painting are one and the same.

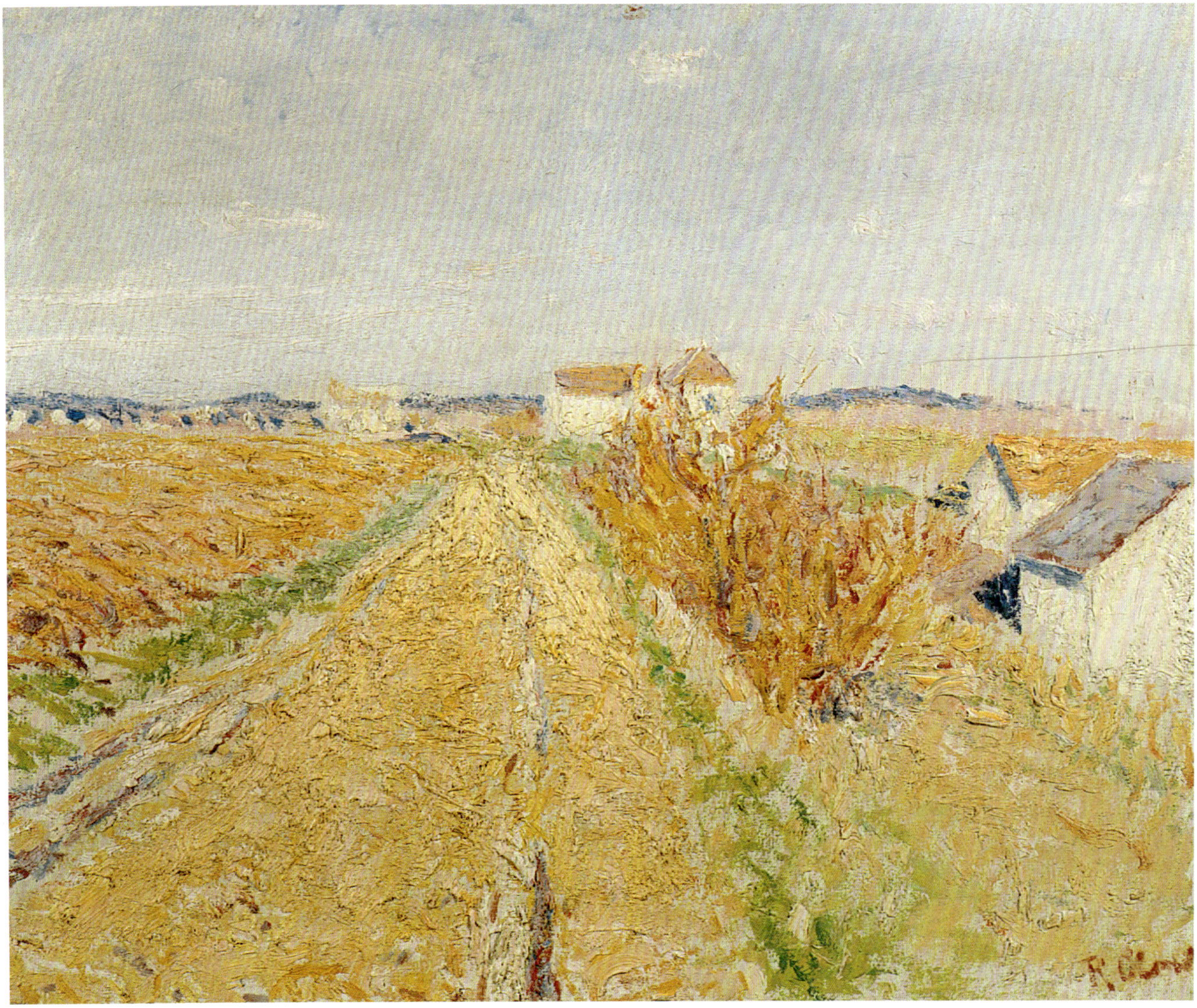

Oil on canvas
72.5 x 90.0 cms.
s.b.r.f. R O'Conor
d.b.r.f. 1890

Prov: Schoneman Galleries, New York; Sotheby's, London, 2 May 1990, no.24 as 'French Landscape'; private collection.

Exh:[?] *Salon des Indépendants* (565) 1890.

Private collection

La lisière du bois

The edge of the wood

This quite remarkable 'Pointillist' painting is unique in O'Conor's oeuvre, revealing an important link between his early Impressionist inspired landscapes painted at Grez-sur-Loing to the south of Paris, and his later Divisionist paintings such as 'Still life with bottles', 1892 (collection Tate Gallery, London). The inspiration here is clearly from Georges Seurat and his fellow Neo-Impressionists, and especially from Signac whose early style it more closely resembles. Seurat's Pointillist pictures, and those of his followers, had been widely exhibited in Paris since 1886[1], co-incidentally the year of O'Conor's arrival in France.

It is evident that O'Conor experimented with different approaches to painting during his first four years in France. For example his two early Impressionist influenced pictures, one signed and dated to the year 1886 (cat. no. 1) and another thought to have been painted circa 1889,(cat. no. 2) stand in contrast to the portrait which he exhibited at the official Salon in 1888.[2] In 1889 he again showed at the official Salon and also at the more progressive Salon des Indépendants, suggesting that there was further experimentation with different styles in that year.

Because this is the only example of O'Conor's work which has been traced to date which so completely embraces the tenets of Seurat's Neo-Impressionism, we may assume that this painting represents a brief flirtation with the style, rather than a sustained commitment to its principles. O'Conor's lively jabbing with the brush has produced a wide variety of marks while still retaining the sense of deliberateness in colour division, distribution, and composition, which was a characteristic of the Neo-Impressionist style in general.

In contrast with Seurat's preference for softer atmospheric effects of light and shade, O'Conor, always the colourist, has chosen his palette to convey the brilliance of light and sunshine as he would have experienced it in the French landscape. It is likely that this work too was painted at Grez-sur-Loing, as O'Conor is known to have been in residence there in 1889 and 1890.

It is also probable that this painting was the one exhibited by O'Conor as 'La Lisière du Bois' in the Salon des Indépendants of 1890. (as No.565). Seurat and Signac were members of the committee for the 1890 Indépendants, having also served the previous year, and there were several other Neo-Impressionist paintings by Luce, Pissarro, and Theo van Rysselberghe in the same exhibition.

1 Seurat had attracted both attention and some controversy at the last Impressionist group exhibition in 1886, when he showed his now famous painting 'Sunday afternoon at la Grand Jatte' (collection of the Art Institute of Chicago). The picture was shown again in the Salon des Indépendants later that year, and the new style was dubbed 'Néo-Impressionnisme' by the distinguished critic Félix Fénéon in an article published in September in '*L'Art Moderne*.' In subsequent years, until Seurat's early death in 1891, numerous Neo-Impressionist paintings were shown at the Salon des Indépendants by artists such as Signac, Camille and Lucien Pissarro, Henri-Edmond Cross, Charles Angrand and Henri Delavallée, a painter/printmaker who had a close connection with Brittany.

2. The painting exhibited at the official Salon in 1888 was 'Portrait de M. Paul Vojelius' (sic), (No.1930). Vogelius was a Danish painter and illustrator whom O'Conor is likely to have met on an early visit to Grez-sur-Loing.

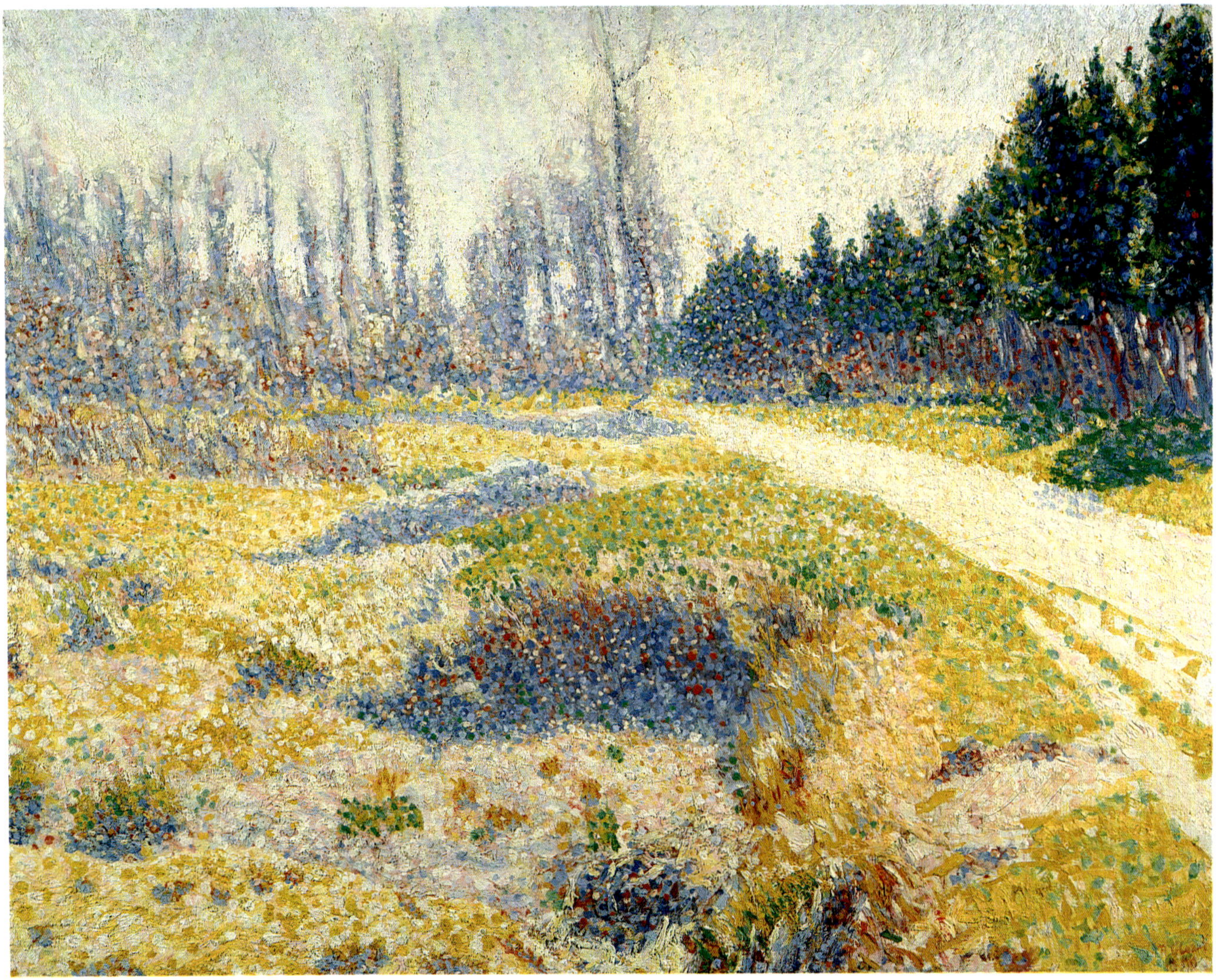

Oil on wooden panel
24.6 x 27.9 cms.
s.b.l.f. O'Conor
d.b.l.f. '92

Prov: Roland, Browse & Delbanco, London, 1962; W.E.Wallace Esq., and the Hon. Mrs.E.A. Wallace; Wooley and Wallis, St. Mary Bourne 1990; private collection.

Exh: London, Roland Browse and Delbanco, 1964 (22).

Lit: Benington, *Celtic Splendor*, Pym's Gallery, London 1985, ill.p.38 Benington (1992) (21).

Private collection

The foaming sea

This small picture is typical of the many marine pictures which O'Conor painted off the Brittany coast, looking from the rocky shoreline out to sea. No horizon line has been included in this picture due to his downward gaze from a high viewing position.

O'Conor's seascapes, particularly those which have been deliberately and heavily worked with the palette knife, often present a more panoramic view than that which exists here. However the more intimate views of sea, rocks, and foam, of which this is a typical example, bring us much closer into contact with the power and force of nature. There is a directness and a sense of energy in the painting of these small works which suggests that O'Conor was inspired by Monet's splendid example in his 1886 Belle-Ile paintings of stormy seas.[1] It may be that O'Conor was himself searching for a similar theme to which he could bring his own personal vision and expressive powers as a painter.

We are also reminded in many of O'Conor's marine pictures, of similar subject matter as painted by his Pont-Aven friends Maufra, Moret and Slewinski. Moret and Maufra preferred the grand view and kept to their Impressionist loyalties while they were in Brittany. Slewinski's turbulent seascapes on the other hand, are closer to O'Conor's in their colour range and in their emotional and expressive qualities. Their close friendship, confirmed in letters exchanged between them, makes it almost certain that they would have traded ideas and opinions about their seascapes.

1 Belle-Ile is a rocky island off the Brittany coast, fully exposed to the force of the Atlantic ocean. See for example Monet's 1886 painting, 'Storm on Belle-Ile' (Private collection, New York).

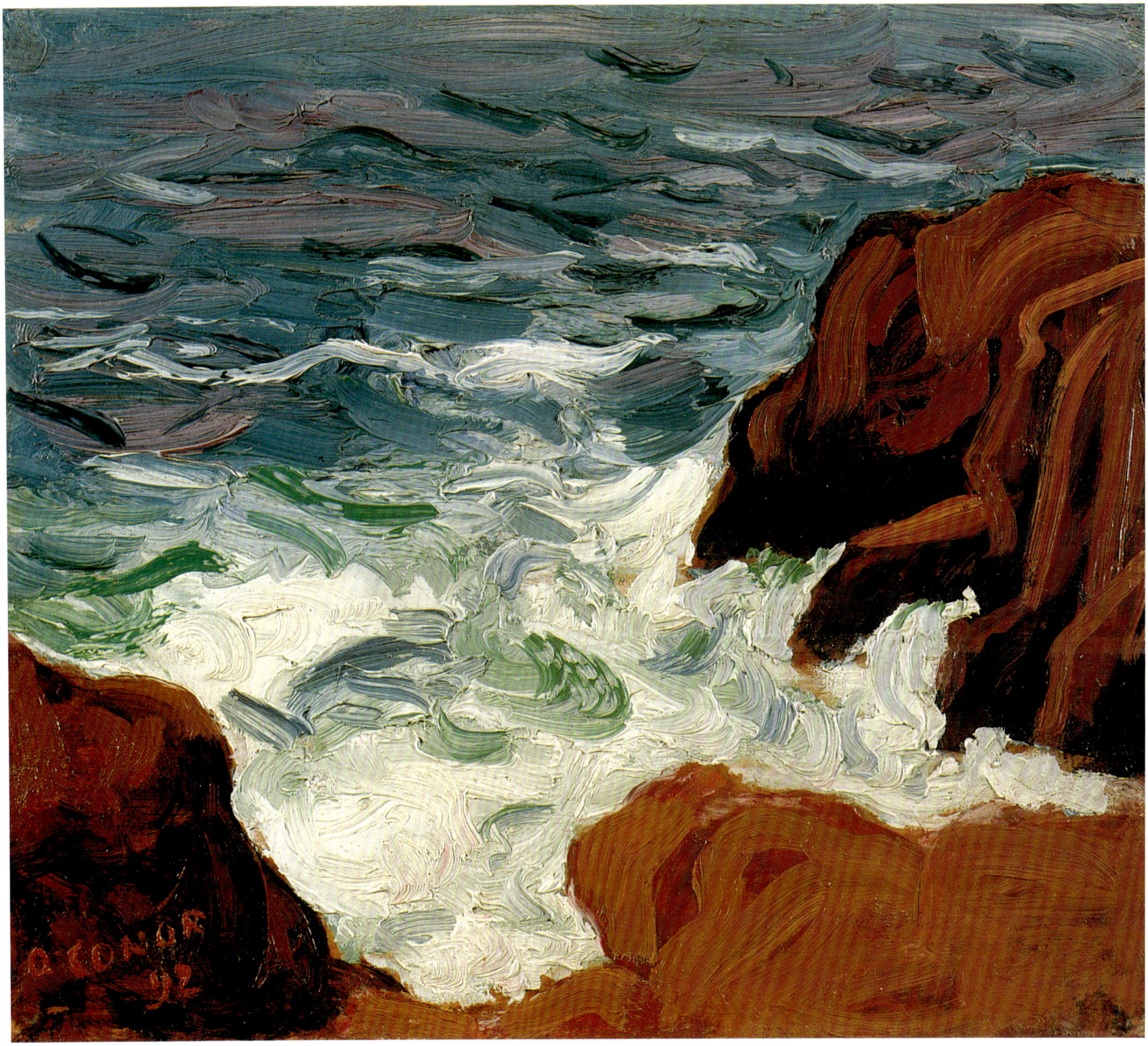
O.CONOR
92

circa. 1893
Oil on panel
30.5 x 33.0 cms
Atelier stamp verso

Prov: Paris, Hôtel Drouot, Vente O'Conor 1956; Mrs. Emmet Dalton 1956; private collection 1994.

Exh: London, Roland, Browse and Delbanco, '*Two Masters of Colour*' 1956 (31); London, Browse and Darby, 1994.

Lit: Sutton, 1960, p.173.

Private collection

Head of a Breton Boy

Although O'Conor is well known as a painter of the landscape through his distinctive heavily striped paintings from Brittany, he also made numerous drawings, etchings, and paintings of the local people. Many of these portraits, especially those painted between 1892-1894 when his use of parallel brush strokes was at its peak, were realised in a similar style. In comparison with some of the dated portraits from 1893, where the striping technique is used quite aggressively, this particular work is more muted and is therefore thought to be early in the series.

O'Conor used this young boy as a model on more than one occasion.[1] He also appears to have been the subject for a drawing with the title 'Tête d'Enfant' which was reproduced in the Parisian review, *L'Ymagier* in 1894, with some help from Alfred Jarry the distinguished writer and art critic. In 1894 when O'Conor was exhibiting at Le Barc de Boutteville's gallery in Paris,[2] Jarry personally collected at least two drawings and an etching plate of O'Conor's from the gallery which were intended for publication in *L'Ymagier*. From correspondence between Jarry and O'Conor[3] it is evident that he also planned to publish an additional drawing of a Breton girl, but this does not appear to have been printed.

1. There is a strong resemblance to the sitter in the painting known as 'Head of a Breton boy with cap', which probably dates from 1893, and to the admittedly more mature looking boy who is the subject of the 1893 picture 'Breton boy in profile'.
2. Le Barc de Boutteville, prior to 1891, had specialised as a dealer in classical and historical paintings, before being persuaded by the impressionist painter Paul Vogler, who had studied with Sisley, to show the best of the new and up and coming artists. His gallery at 47 rue Peletier in Montmartre, presented a series of group exhibitions under the general title 'Peintres Impressionistes et Symbolistes'. O'Conor exhibited in the sixth, seventh, and eighth exhibitions in this series in March, July, and November of 1894, and in 1895. Other exhibitors in the sixth exhibition included Anquetin, Bonnard, Filiger, Gauguin, Loiseau, Serusier, and Vuillard. Among O'Conor's six exhibits was one entitled 'Jeune Paysan' (No.42).
3. Jarry wrote to O'Conor - 'J'ai bien trouvé chez le Barc l'eau-forte et les deux dessins qui m'ont plaît beaucoup, surtout la tête de Bretonne. Dans L'Ymagier qui va paraître vous verrez l'eau forte en tête de numéro, ainsi que la figure d'enfant. Undated letter, presumably 1894. Private collection, France.

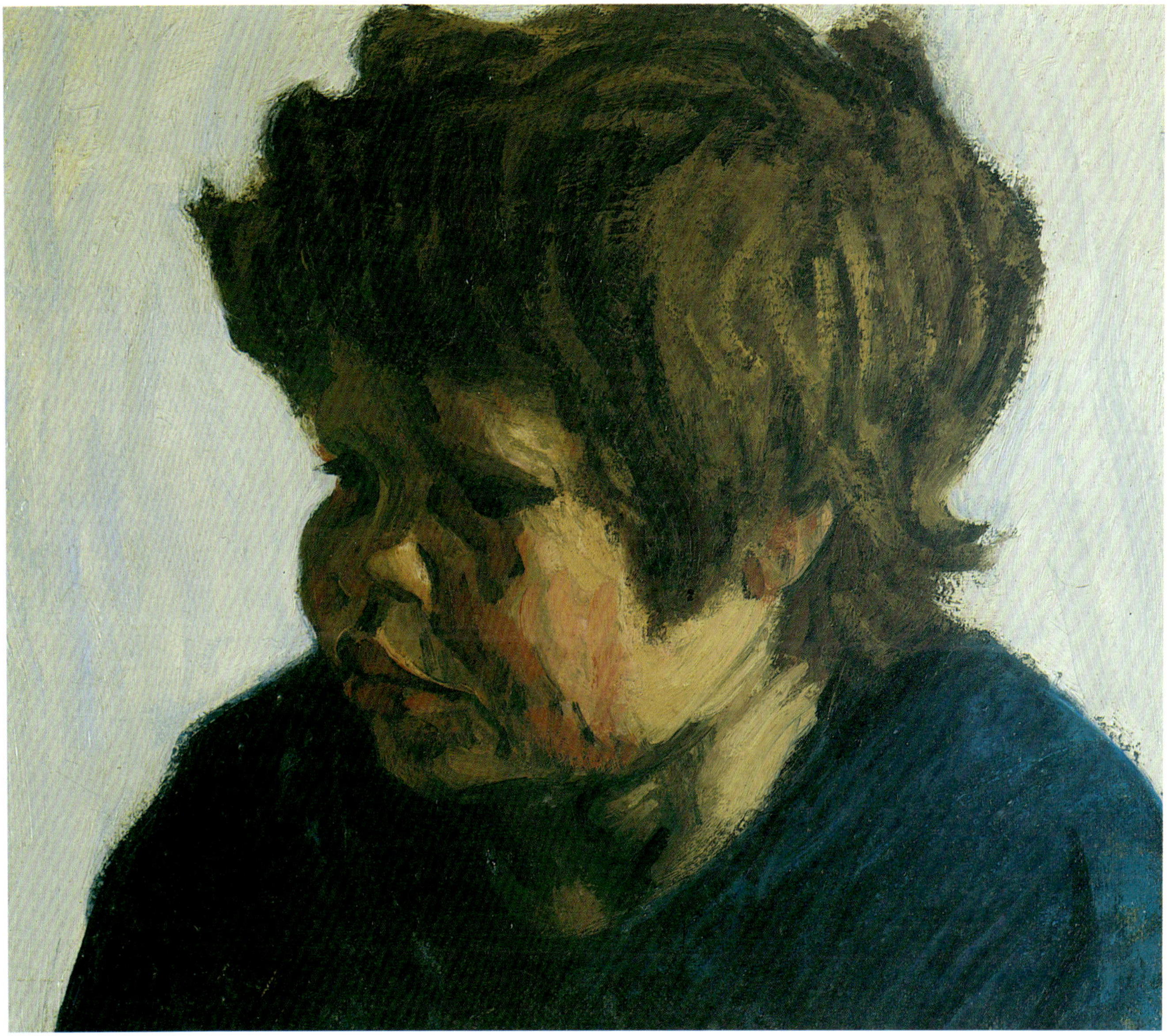

circa. 1894
Oil on canvas
81.3 x 64.8 cms.
Signed: verso, R. O'Conor
Insc: verso, L'approche de Lezaven Pont-Aven

Prov: Roderic O'Conor to Francis Chadwick at Grez-sur-Loing; then by descent to his grand-daughter Madame C. Colomb; private collection 1983.

Exh: Paris, *Salon d'Automne*, 1905 (1177); Pont-Aven, *Roderic O'Conor 1860-1940*, Musée de Pont-Aven, 1984 (35) ill.; London, Belfast, Dublin, Manchester, *Roderic O'Conor 1860-1940*, 1985 (17) ill. p.42.

Lit: Benington 1985, pp.257-8, ill. p.258; Johnston 1984 p.43 ill.; Johnston 1985, p.69 ill.; Benington 1992 (40).

Private collection

L'approche de Lezaven

Near Lezaven

The buildings known to the Pont-Aven artists as the Lezaven farm are just visible in the upper right background of this picture. Situated on high ground above Pont-Aven, and some distance back from the road, the farm could be approached from the village by this footpath through the trees which partially concealed the buildings from general view.

The first generation of Pont-Aven artists were given access to these outbuildings by a local notary as early as 1866, in response to their needs for a studio space. The studio was communal and its location gave it much privacy. Gauguin is known to have painted there, and O'Conor also painted more than one canvas in and around this area. [1]

Although this painting was not exhibited until 1905 two years after Gauguin's death, it is tempting, because of the obvious Gauguin influence, to date it to the year 1894 when he and O'Conor were in contact in Pont-Aven.

The comparisons to be made with Gauguin are most obvious in the colour range, but are also evident in O'Conor's non-naturalistic and rather schematic interpretation of subject matter drawn from nature and his own experience. O'Conor's use of the tree trunks as a type of visual screen to reduce the spatial reading is a pictorial device borrowed directly from Gauguin. This flattening of space and emphasis on the decorative contour was a general characteristic of the work of the School of Pont-Aven artists.

The rather schematic forms in O'Conor's painting suggest that it was probably completed in the studio, and this more than anything may have contributed to its slightly non-naturalistic appearance. Gauguin frequently worked this way, and encouraged his followers to do likewise, although the practice caused some confusion among his group, some of whom, including Sérusier, were left unclear as to what the role of nature and the observation of nature should be.[2]

1. O'Conor also painted a different view of the farm from above and beyond the buildings which is signed and dated 1894 and although it is rather more fluidly painted than this work, with more medium in the oil paint, there is a relationship between the two paintings in the brushwork describing the vegetation and undergrowth beneath the trees. See O'Conor's painting 'La Ferme de Lezaven', 1894, in the collection of the National Gallery of Ireland, Dublin.
2. Sérusier, Paul *ABC de la peinture*, Paris (1950) p.39. 'Ce que m'a surtout embarrassé, le voilà: quelle part la nature doit-elle avoir dans l'oeuvre? Où s'arrêter? Enfin, au point de vue matériel de l'exécution, faut-il travailler d'après nature, ou seulement regarder de se souvenir?'

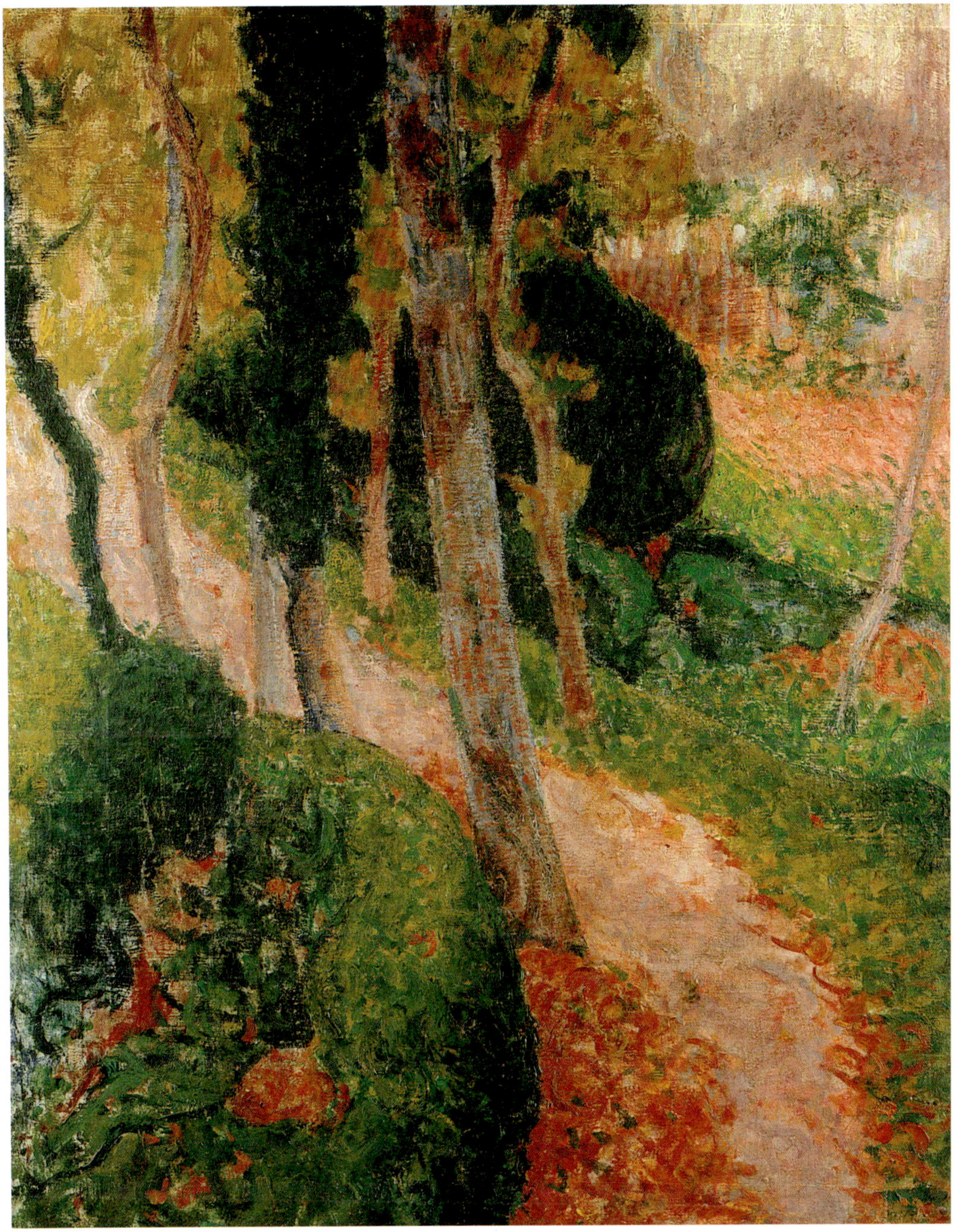

circa. 1897-98
oil on canvas
92.4 x 73.0 cms
Insc:verso Pont-Aven à
Lezaven
R. O'Conor 1898

Prov: Roland, Browse, and Delbanco, London; Schoneman Galleries, New York 1960; private collection U.S.A.; Pym's Gallery, London 1994; private collection.

Exh: London, Roland, Browse and Delbanco, *French pictures of the 19th. and 20th. century*, 1958 (17) as 'Red road at Pont-Aven'; London, Belfast, Dublin, Manchester *Roderic O'Conor 1860-1940,* 1985, (No.20) ill.

Lit: Sutton, 1960, p. 168 (ill.); O'Brian 1982, pp.15-16; Campbell, Julian, *The Irish Impressionists* Dublin 1984, p.99; Benington 1985, pp.257, 260 (ill.); Benington 1992 (53) as 'Village Scene'

Private collection

Landscape

This loosely worked painting of a cluster of houses is quite remarkable for O'Conor's use of such a vivid and contrasting colour range. The directness of his approach where drawing and painting have really become the one activity, was typical of his method of beginning a painting. Energetic brush marks and richness of colour contrasts are combined to give a strongly expressionist reading to this work which is quite advanced for a late nineteenth century painting. As the noted art critic Clive Bell later wrote about O'Conor 'these pictures painted at the beginning of the century are sometimes oddly like what daring young men were to paint ten years later'.[1]

In spite of the inscription on the stretcher bar, it is more likely that this painting belongs to that period between 1895 and the beginning of 1899 when O'Conor was living in Rochefort-en-Terre in Morbihan. Rocheford served as a place of retreat and contemplation for him after Gauguin's departure for the South Seas in 1895. There is nothing in the environs of Rochefort itself which would specifically suggest such a colour range, although the vigour of the brush work in this painting is also apparent in his 1897 seascapes.

It is O'Conor's boldness in the colour range which distinguishes this painting, and indeed it might almost be assumed that its primary allegiance was to Fauvism. The Fauvists however did not emerge as a group until the 1905 Salon d'Automne exhibition, so that any similarities are based on colour associations alone, without the evidence of any shared theoretical concerns.

It is interesting however to note that the Parisian dealer Clovis Sagot, who actively promoted the Fauvists, did make an approach to O'Conor in 1903 with an invitation to exhibit in his gallery.[2] O'Conor did not take up the offer although the reasons for turning Sagot down, other than his known dislike of dealers and commercial galleries in general, are not known.

There is no doubt however, that a painting such as this does appear in retrospect to be somewhat ahead of its time, and it may be that it was just such a work which led the noted English painter Matthew Smith, who met O'Conor in 1919, to conclude that O'Conor was 'fauve before the fauves'. Indeed the colour range here is echoed in many of Smith's own landscapes painted in Cornwall in 1920, and it is not too difficult to see from the evidence of this work why Smith should refer to O'Conor in later years as 'Mon Maître'.[3]

1. Bell, Clive, *Old Friends*, London 1956 p.165.
2. Letter from Clovis Sagot to Roderic O'Conor dated 20 November 1903, in which he commented favourably on O'Conor's work at the Salon d'Automne. Private collection, France.
3. London, Barbican Art Gallery, *Matthew Smith*, exhibition catalogue, 1983 p.22.

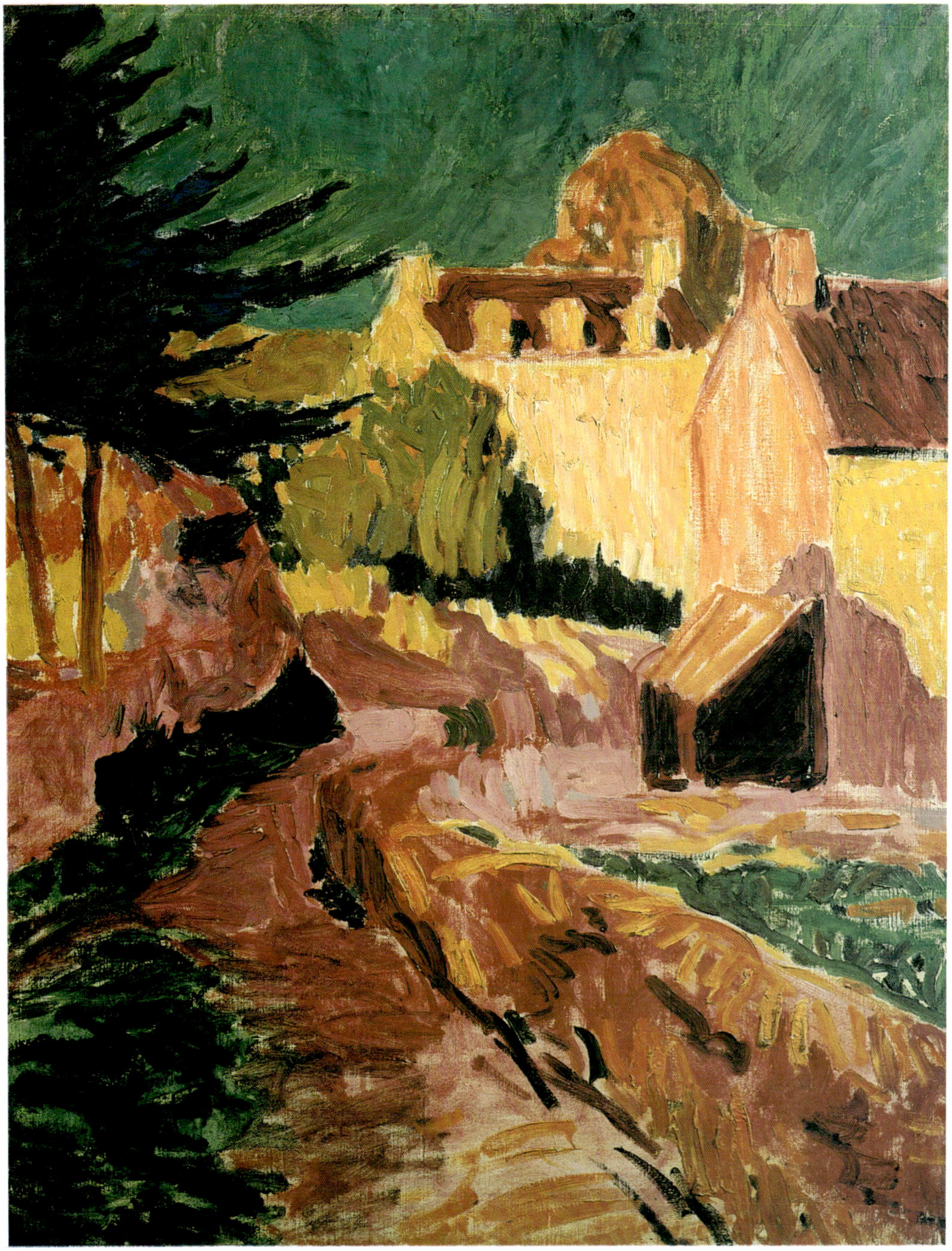

circa. 1898
Oil on canvas
54.2 x 64.5 cms
Atelier stamp verso

Prov: Paris, Hôtel Drouot, Vente O'Conor, 1956; Roland, Browse, and Delbanco, London; J. Stebbings; Bonhams, London, 16 July 1992; Pyms Gallery, London; private collection.

Exh: London, Roland, Browse & Delbanco 1961 (10).

Lit: Benington, 1992 (67).

Private collection

Blue sea and rocks, Brittany

Due to O'Conor's high viewing position above the rocks, almost all of his seascapes have in common the use of a high horizon line. This compositional arrangement gave him numerous opportunities to depict the changing moods of the surging sea as it foamed around the rocky shoreline below. In this painting the sea is relatively calm while in other works a more active sea has been vigorously painted with a well charged brush, giving O'Conor great scope for his powers of expression and for the directness and immediacy of his painting technique.

This particular outcrop of rock appears in several of O'Conor's seascapes with marginal changes in each painting depending on the fullness of the tide, and the amount of turbulence in the sea. The light also varies in the seascapes from full sunlight with maximum contrasts to the softer golden tones of a setting sun. In painting so many seascapes, and by returning at different times to the same outcrop of rock, O'Conor may well have been following the example set by Monet in his Belle-Isle-en-Mer pictures of rocks and sea at Port Croton, which he painted in 1886 and which were exhibited in 1887 and 1889 at Georges Petit's gallery in Paris.

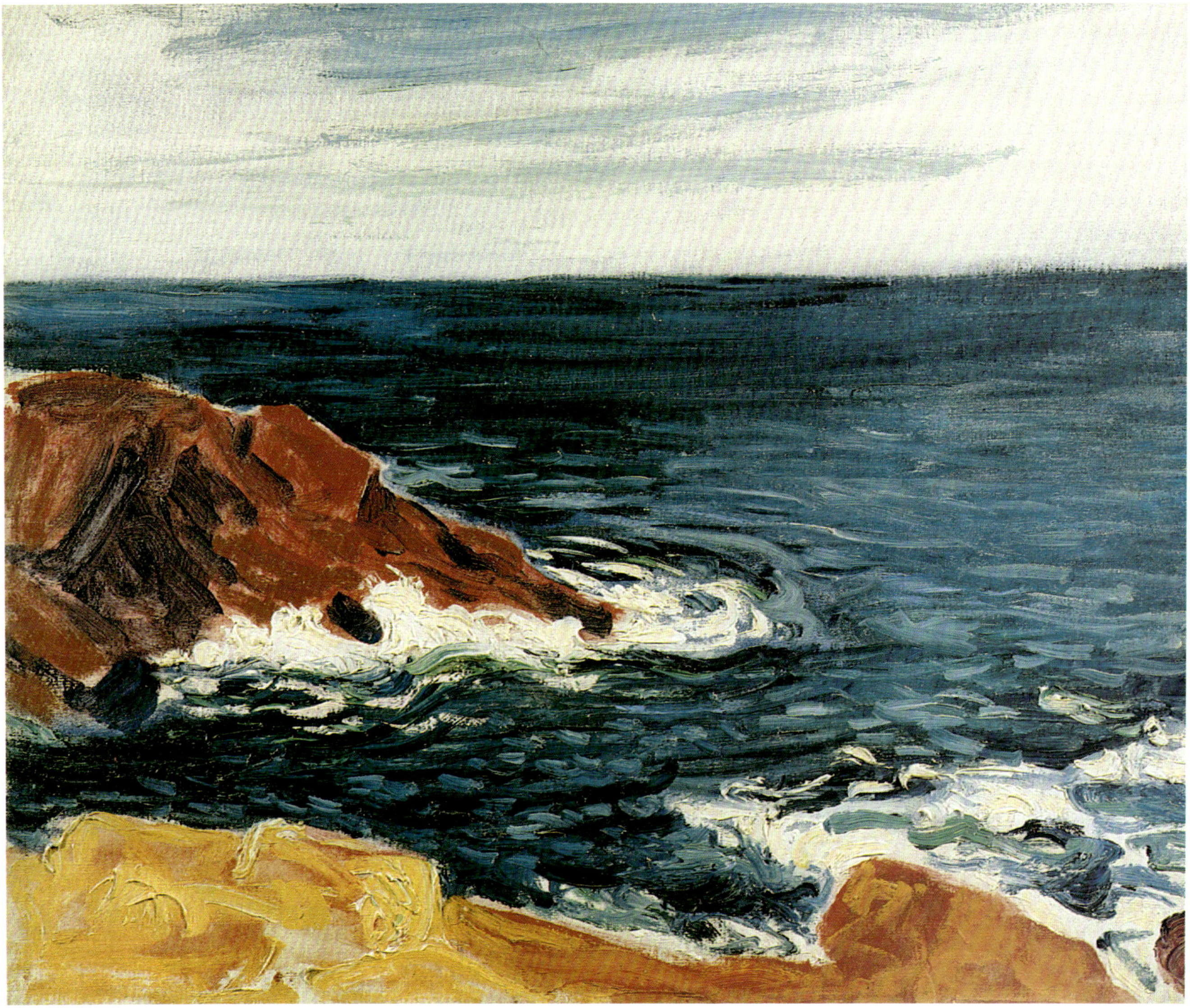

Paysage avec moutons

Landscape with sheep

circa. 1900
Oil on canvas
73.0 x 92.1 cms
s.b.r.f. O'Conor
Atelier stamp verso
Insc:verso, indistinctly on the stretcher, 'Coucher de sol..[Bretagne] and signed Roderic O'Conor

Prov: Hôtel Drouot, Paris, Vente O'Conor, 1956; Musée du Petit Palais, Genève; Pym's Gallery, London; private collection.

Exh: [?] Paris, *Salon des Indépendants*, 1905 (3103); Genève, Petit Palais, *Peintres Brittaniques du XXème siècle*, 1980; Pont-Aven, Musée de Pont-Aven, *Roderic O'Conor, 1860-1940* 1984 (No. 33) ill. p.42; London, Belfast, Dublin, Manchester, *Roderic O'Conor, 1860-1940*, 1985 (No. 51) ill. p.84.

Lit: Petit Palais Genève, 629 Oeuvres de Renoir à Picasso, 1980, ill.; Benington 1992 (85).

Private collection

Paintings of rural life and of peasants working in the fields herding their animals were common subjects for numerous 19th. century French artists including Charles Émile Jacque, and perhaps best known of all, Jean-Francois Millet. Although much more radical in his style and technique than either of these romantic realist artists, O'Conor in this composition takes a subject which both of them had painted frequently, and creates a painting with a quite remarkable sense of mood and atmosphere.

In many of his paintings, and frequently in his etchings, O'Conor presents us with a view towards the light source, in this case the setting sun, with the main subject matter lit from behind. It is this viewpoint which adds drama and atmosphere to this distinctive painting. In the background the paint has been applied thickly and built up almost to an excess using the palette knife to give rich impasto effects, with O'Conor showing his innate ability to exploit the physicality of oil paint in service of his subject matter. The pronounced texture of the dragged palette knife surface stands in marked contrast to the sensitivity and understatement of the brush work defining the flock of sheep. The rich colouration gives the painting an inner glow consistent with evening light, and the sheep which are suggested rather than explicitly stated, seem to emerge slowly towards the viewer from the dimly lit middle ground.

The inscription on the stretcher bar suggests that this may be the painting entitled 'Coucher de soleil' which O'Conor exhibited at the 1905 Salon des Indépendants. There are also shared characteristics with several other similarly painted works which are thought to date to his Brittany years. Whatever their precise date, they represent an exceptional tour de force in their vision and in their technique.

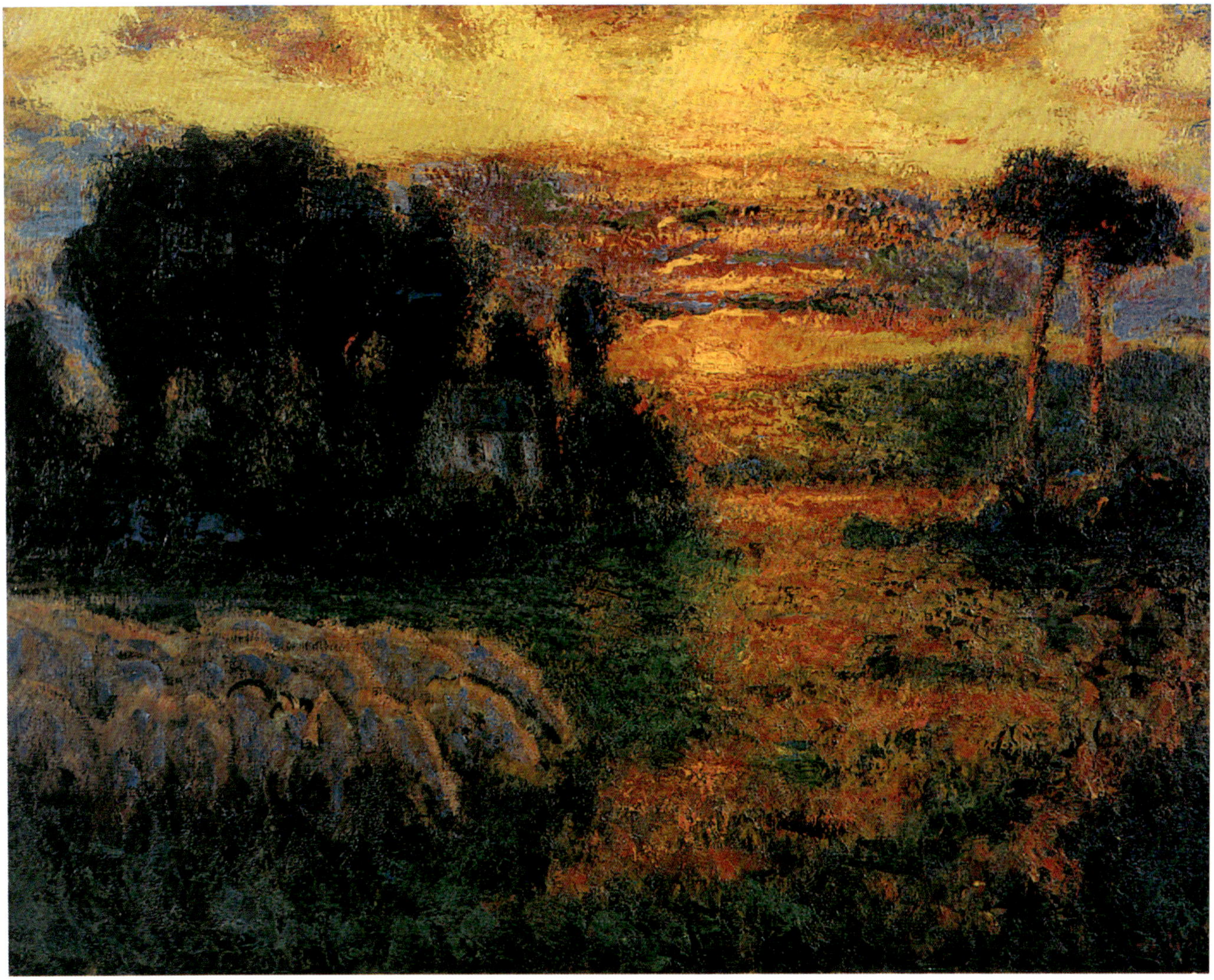

circa. 1900
Oil on canvas
73.0 x 92.1 cms.
s.b.r.f. O'Conor [?]
Atelier stamp verso

Prov: Hotel Drouot, Paris, Vente O'Conor, 1956; Musée de Petit Palais, Genève; Pym's Gallery, London; private collection.

Exh: Genève, Petit Palais, *Peintres Brittaniques du XXe Siecle,* 1980; Pont-Aven, Musée de Pont-Aven, *Roderic O'Conor 1860-1940*, 1984 (No. 32) ill.; London, Belfast, Dublin, Manchester, *Roderic O'Conor 1860-1940,* 1985 (No. 52) ill.

Lit: Benington 1992 (91).

Private collection

Personnages avec cheval

Figures with horse

Although the treatment in this painting is uniquely O'Conor's, the introduction of the two female figures, one clothed and the other nude and in a submissive pose, suggests that there was an intention in this picture to deal with symbolic and overtly sensual references. The clothed figure appears to be trying to mount, or possibly to control a plunging animal which is probably a horse. During the Renaissance the horse was frequently used as a symbol of lust, and its association with erotic power and sexual prowess continued to feature in the work of many nineteenth century Romantic painters.

In O'Conor's painting there are also strong echoes, largely because of the horse's posture, of Gauguin's 1898 picture 'Le Cheval Blanc' although this work was not exhibited in Paris until 1906, three years after Gauguin's death. If not inspired directly by knowledge of Gauguin's picture, then this work by O'Conor shows a remarkable degree of 'rapprochement', confirming the extent to which he knew and understood Gauguin's artistic personality.

It is known that Gauguin had been referring to photographs of works of art as sources for some of the figures in his paintings, from at least 1891. Some of this was probably shared with O'Conor when he and Gauguin were together in Pont-Aven in 1894.[1] Gauguin appropriated the image of the horse in his 1898 painting from a photograph of a Phidias carving on the west frieze of the Parthenon.[2] The horse in O'Conor's painting is a reversal of Gauguin's, but could O'Conor's inclusion of a foreground figure be an oblique reference to the rider in front of the horse in the same carving? Even if this should be the case, it has to be acknowledged that the original figure and its derivative do not share strong visual similarities. In the Phidias carving the rider is male and in O'Conor's painting the figure is clearly female. Her voluminous dress is however similar to the garments worn by women depicted on the Parthenon frieze, which of course also had an abundance of rearing and plunging horses, bulls, and centaurs on its facades. The similarity to Gauguin's painting, and to figures carved on the frieze, may be purely co-incidental of course but certainly the pose of the unclothed figure to the right is very 'Gauguinesque', and quite unlike any others in O'Conor's work.

If not from the frieze or from 'Le Cheval Blanc' what other possible sources may have motivated O'Conor to paint this work? It is perhaps more plausible that some inspiration came directly from Gauguin's pictures which he began to send back to Paris from Tahiti for exhibition in years subsequent to 1896.[3] One particular group shown in Paris in 1898 included several pictures of dimly lit figures in a dark setting underneath sombre trees. For example, Gauguin's painting 'Te pape nave nave', (collection of the National Gallery of Art, Washington, D.C.) with its evening light from a setting sun throwing the trunks of background trees into silhouette, shares a similar mysterious almost sinister atmosphere, to that which has been created here by O'Conor.

1. O'Conor must surely have known that Gauguin's 1892 painting 'Te Nave Nave Fenua', which he bought at Gauguin's auction in Paris in 1895, was derived from a photograph which he had in his possession of the sculptured frieze from the Buddist temple at Borobudur.
2. See Kane, William M. 'Gauguin's Le Cheval Blanc: Sources and Syncretic Meanings', *Burlington Magazine* Vol.CVIII No. 760 (July 1966) for a detailed analysis of Gauguin's sources. See also Dorival, Bernard 'Sources of the art of Gauguin from Java, Egypt, and Ancient Greece', *Burlington Magazine* April 1951 pp. 118-22, and July 1951 p.237
3. From Seguin's correspondence we know that O'Conor made a visit to Paris late in October or early in November of 1898, and might very well have had the opportunity to see this group of Gauguin's pictures. Seguin also made him aware of the Gauguin exhibition in a later letter when he wrote: 'Savez-vous que Gauguin fait une exposition de nouvelles oeuvres chez Vollard, avez-vous su des nouvelles de ce bon vieux, que sais-je?' Seguin to O'Conor letter No. 45, 1 December 1898, Sutton, Puget, Boyle-Turner eds; *Une Vie de Bohême*, Lausanne, 1989.

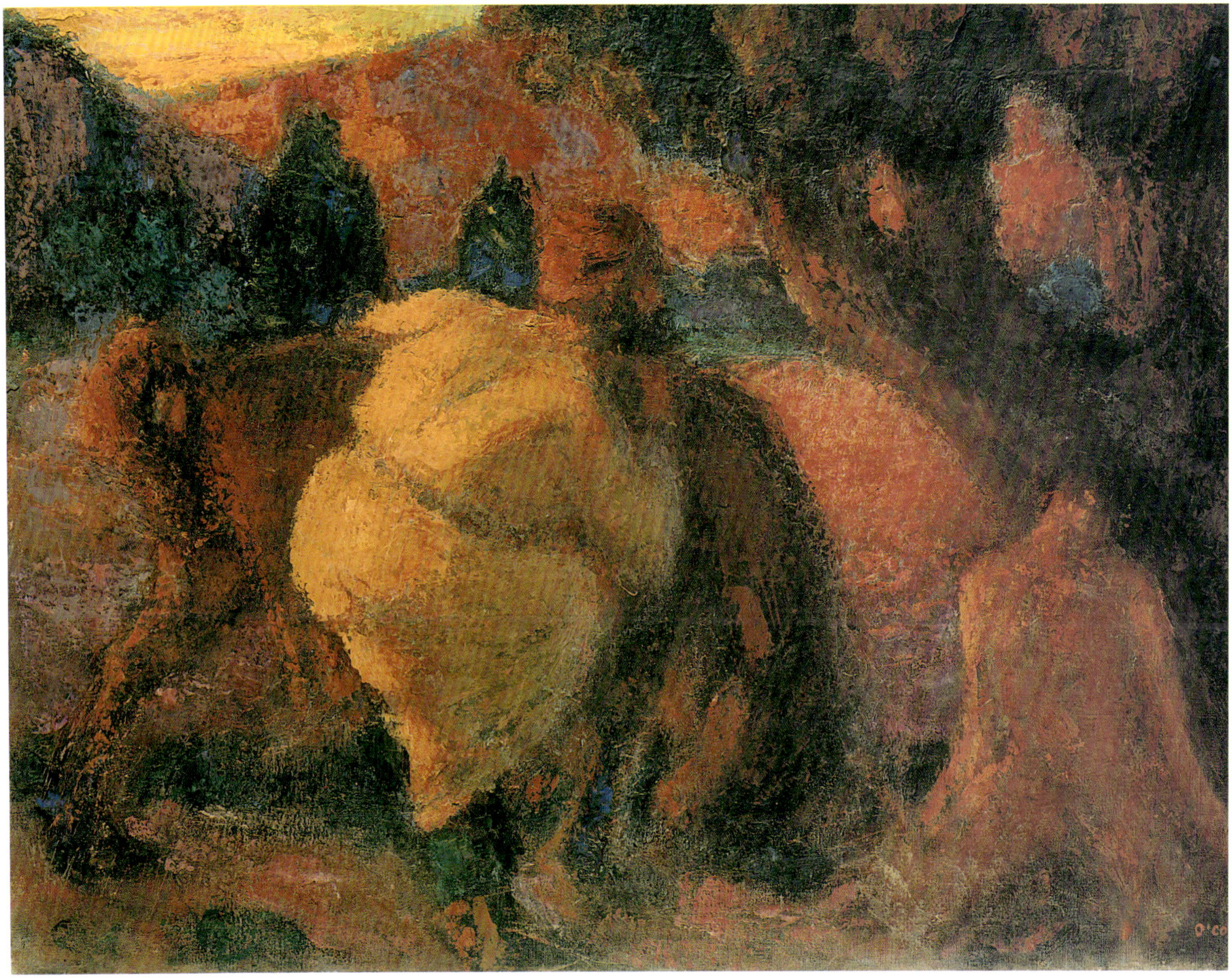

Oil on canvas
91.5 x 73.6 cms.
s.b.l.f. O'Conor
d.b.l.f.1903

Prov: Donated by the artist 1904.

Exh: [?] Paris, *Salon d'Automne,* 1903 (422); London, Guildhall, *Exhibition of works by Irish painters,* 1904 (23) ill.; Dublin, Municipal Gallery of Modern Art, 1908 (30) p.4; Brussels, Musée d'Art Ancien, *Exposition d'art Irlandais,* 1930 (124); Ohio, Columbus Gallery of Fine Arts; Museum of Arts, Toledo; Art Museum, St. Louis, *Aspects of Irish Art,* 1974 (56) ill.; Dublin, Douglas Hyde Gallery, *The Peasant in French 19th. Century Art,* 1980 (78); Pont-Aven, *Roderic O'Conor 1860-1940,* Musée de Pont-Aven, 1984 (39) ill. p.25 & 44; Dublin, Hugh Lane Municipal Gallery of Modern Art, *The City's Art,* 1984; London, Belfast, Dublin, Manchester, *Roderic O'Conor 1860-1940,* 1985 (43) ill. p.81.

Lit: Sutton 1960, p.194; Arnold, *A concise history of Irish art,* London 1977, (109) ill. p.118; Campbell, *The Peasant in French 19th. Century Art,* 1980, p.188; Johnston 1984 p.45; Benington 1985, p. 259-261 ill. p.261; Johnston 1985 p.81, ill.; Benington, Nov. 1987, *Journal of the American Medical Association,* p. 2474, ill. cover; Benington 1992 (105); *Images and Insights,* Hugh Lane Municipal Gallery of Modern Art, Dublin 1993 p.74, ill. p.75; Murphy 1992, ill. p.13

Hugh Lane Municipal Gallery of Modern Art, Dublin.

Une Jeune Bretonne

Young Breton girl

O'Conor painted several portraits of this young Breton girl when he was in Pont-Aven.[1] In contrast with the aloof and rather haughty expression on the same girl's face in the painting known as 'Bretonne' (Murnaghan collection, U.S.A.), this particular portrait has an added intensity of gaze and a distant look which is both serene and melancholy.

We know from the traditions of everyday life among the Breton people that she is in mourning, a state which is confirmed by the lowering of the two long 'ailes' which are normally pinned to her 'head-dress' or coiffe. A black shawl covers the normally visible wide white starched collar which rests on her shoulders.

The painting also represents a return to a more academic style which gradually began to reappear in O'Conor's work as Gauguin's circle in Pont-Aven slowly drifted apart after he left to return to the South Seas. There are some passages in this portrait which refer back to O'Conor's use of parallel stripes of colour in his earlier paintings, but by the time this work was painted these references had become muted.

The painting is of particular interest as it was included by Hugh Lane in the exhibition of work by Irish artists which he organised for the London Guildhall in 1904. While the portrait would have been in keeping with the work of Lavery, Osborne, and Orpen, who were also represented in the exhibition, it remains a rather conservative choice in comparison to O'Conor's more adventurous and experimental work from 1892-'94. It was possibly the case that Hugh Lane, who only began to buy Impressionist paintings in 1905, was not quite ready for paintings as radical as O'Conor's 1892 series of Breton landscapes for example.

On the other hand if Lane did not actually visit O'Conor, who was then still based in Pont Aven, but chose this painting from the 1903 Salon d'Automne exhibition where it was probably exhibited, he may not have been aware of the range of experimentation in O'Conor's more expressive and adventurous paintings from ten years earlier.[2] We can only speculate on what the impact of these earlier paintings would have been if they had been included in the 1904 exhibition in London. In this context it is perhaps worth noting that the exhibition organised by Roger Fry, which first established the use of the term 'Post-Impressionism', and which presented Gauguin, van Gogh and Cezanne among others to an unsuspecting British public, was not shown in London until 1910.

1. See for example "Bretonne" c. 1903, *Roderic O'Conor 1860-1940,* Barbican Art Gallery London, 1985. (42)
2. In the 1903 Salon d'Autumne O'Conor exhibited three paintings. 421. *Montigny-sur-Loing paysage;* 492. *Jeune Bretonne; 423 Nature Morte*

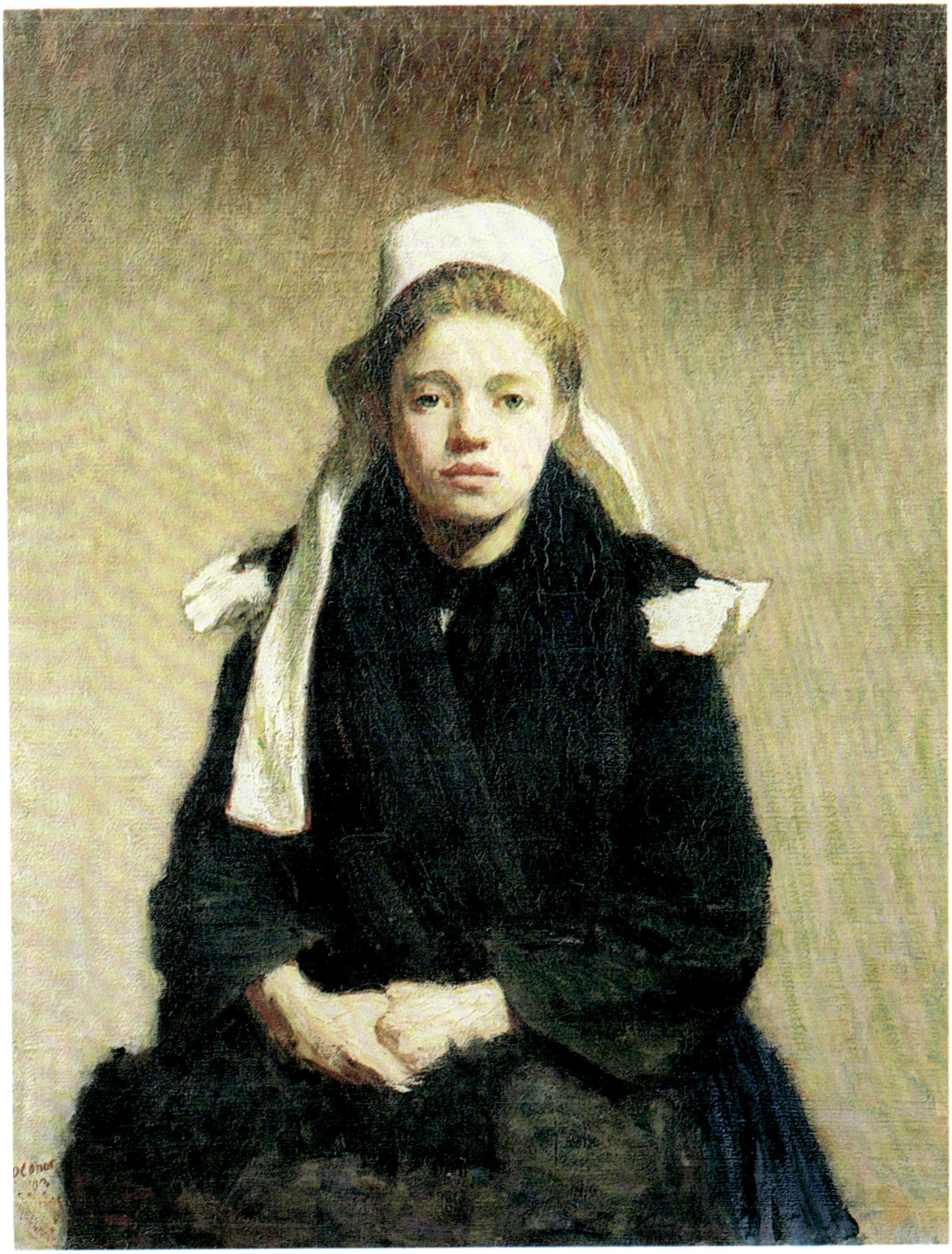

circa. 1905-'06
Oil on canvas
54.3 x 65.4 cms.
s.b.l.f. R.O'Conor
d.b.l.f. 1907
Insc: on the stretcher - Boulevard Raspail Roderic O'Conor No.1.

Prov: Waddington Galleries, London 1958; Galerie Urban, Paris 1959; J. Borges; Crane Kalman Gallery, London.

Exh: Paris, *Salon des Indépendants,* 1906 (3732); London, Waddington Galleries, *Three Painters - Ivon Hitchens, Jack B. Yeats, Roderic O'Conor,* 1958 (21); Dublin, National Gallery of Ireland, *The Irish Impressionists*, 1984 (102) ill. p.245; London, Belfast, Dublin, Manchester, *Roderic O'Conor 1860-1940,* 1985 (44) p.82 ill.

Lit:Sutton 1960, p.172 ill. p.195; Johnston 1985 (44) p.82 ill.; Benington 1992, (112) p.96 ill.

Hugh Lane Municipal Gallery of Modern Art, Dublin.

Boulevard Raspail

Boulevard Raspail

The inscription on the stretcher bar of this canvas identifies the work as one of a group of seven paintings which O'Conor exhibited at the Salon des Indépendants in 1906. The date on the bottom left of the canvas is therefore incorrect and it is likely to have been added later, as this work would probably have been painted in the winter of 1905/06 to have been included in the March 1906 exhibition. Included in the Indépendants that year were paintings by Bernard, Bonnard, Braque, Dufy, Matisse, Rouault, Signac, van Dongen and Vuillard, among others.

The Boulevard Raspail, was then, and still is a busy Parisian thoroughfare which links the Boulevard St.Germain with the Boulevard Montparnasse, crossing over the much narrower rue du Cherche-Midi within 600 metres of the building in which O'Conor had his studio. Unlike many of his contemporaries, O'Conor rarely painted the urban environment or the great boulevards of Paris so that this subject is unusual in his oeuvre.

Depicting a night scene, the painting's sombre and mysterious mood is enhanced by the colour range and the inclusion of the cloaked figures. There appears to be building work or construction in progress, judging from the inclusion of the two tall tower like structures which run from top to bottom in the painting, and from what appears to be a mound of rubble on the ground beneath.

The rather sinister mood and the more fluid brushstrokes suggest some influence from Edward Munch who had been an exhibitor at the Salon des Indépendants from 1896-1898 and again in 1903. Included among the eight works shown by Munch in 1903 were two night scenes which may very well have been an inspiration for O'Conor in this picture. We know that O'Conor was familiar with Munch's paintings through a reference made by Seguin in one of his letters [1] and he owned two of Munch's lithographs.[2]

In spite of the inclusion of the elongated brush strokes, the painting technique is quite different to the heavier impasto surfaces of O'Conor's earlier striped works from Brittany. Much more medium has been added to the paint which is then brushed and blended on the canvas in a wet on wet technique, recalling the methods used in some of his vigorous and expressive seascapes from 1897/98. One of these seascapes 'Marée Montante' was exhibited with 'Boulevard Raspail' in the 1906 Indépendants exhibition.

1. Seguin to O'Conor, in a letter written from Châteaulin, Finistère on 9 April 1903. O'Conor must have drawn Seguin's attention to Munch's paintings at the 1903 Salon des Indépendants. Seguin replied: 'Je n'ai vue qu'une toile de Munch et je ne l'ai pas aimé'.
2. The Munch lithographs were among a number of prints sold at the dispersal sale of O'Conor's collection, including his own paintings, which was held at Hôtel Drouot in Paris on 6/7 February 1956

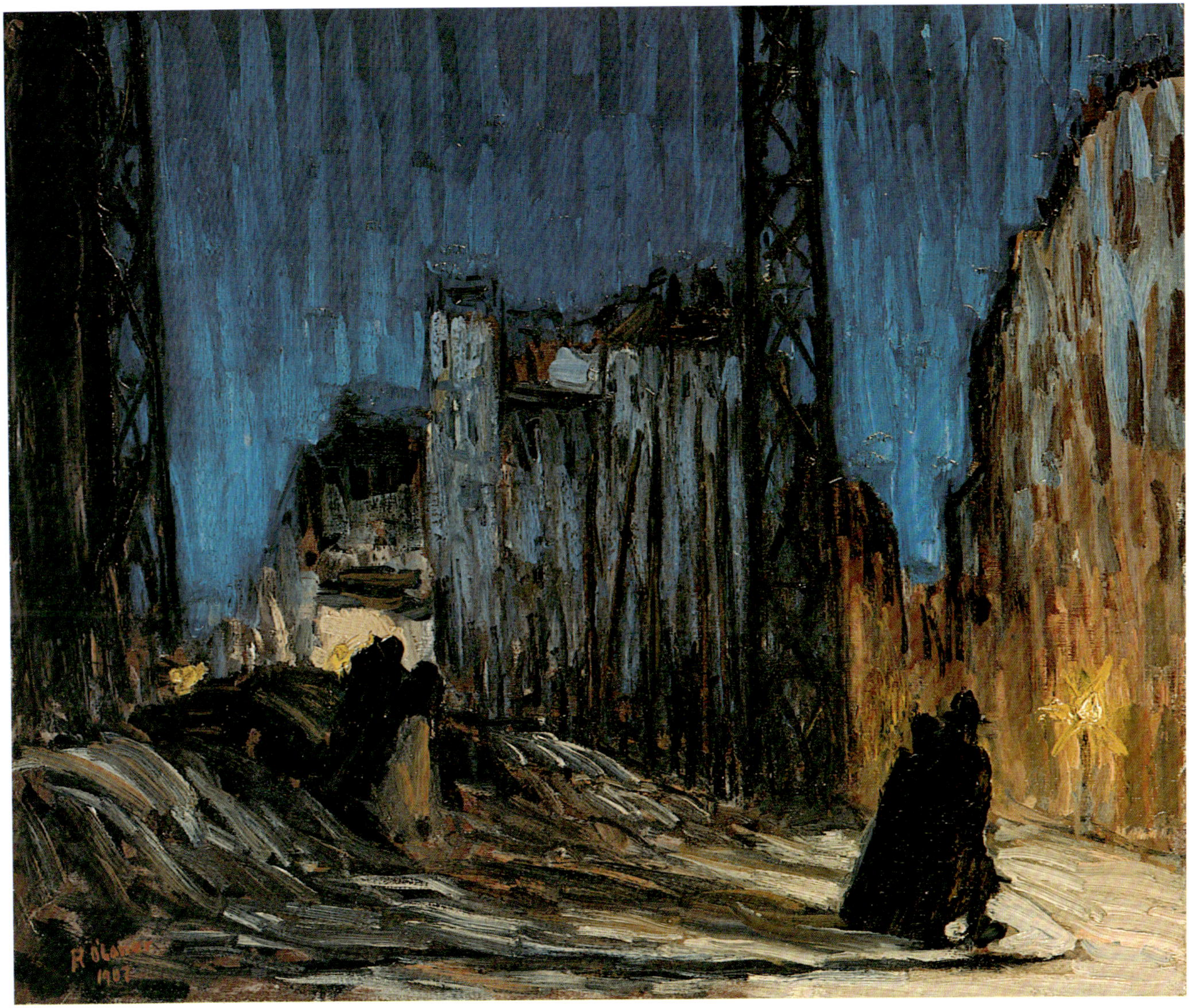

Oil on canvas
64.8 x 81.3 cms
s.b.r.f. R O'Conor
d.b.r.f. 1907 or 1909
atelier stamp verso
Insc: Verso, on the canvas 'Italian light'.

Prov: Paris, Hôtel Drouot, Vente O'Conor 1956; Crane Kalman Gallery, London; Bernard G. Gore 1961; Sean O'Criadain 1976; private collection.

Exh: [?] Paris, *Salon d'Automne*, 1909 as 'Le drap Blanc' (1318)

Lit: Benington, (130) as 'Le drap blanc'.

Private collection

Reclining female nude

This painting is also known as 'Le drap blanc', but in the absence of any inscription confirming this on the back of the painting, we cannot be certain that it is the work of the same name which O'Conor exhibited at the Salon d'Automne in 1909 (1318).

O'Conor painted many such nudes in his Montparnasse studio after 1904. All his favourite props are here - the divan loosely draped with a sheet in front of the studio window with the model posed in such a way that the warm sunlight falls over the contours of her body. Although the pose has obviously been set by the painter, the model's downard glance at her raised hand captures a personal gesture which gives added interest to an otherwise straightforward composition.

Always interested in bright light and contrasting colour in his paintings, O'Conor in this work introduces a near complimentary contrast in the colour range between orange and violet which greatly enriches the visual effect. The painting also reveals the usual variety in his painting methods with some areas little more than lightly stained in contrast with those passages where the brush marks are clearly visible in the heavier paint. O'Conor rarely overworked a painting and in the treatment of the head, for example, we see how effective his understatement of the details has been in this context.

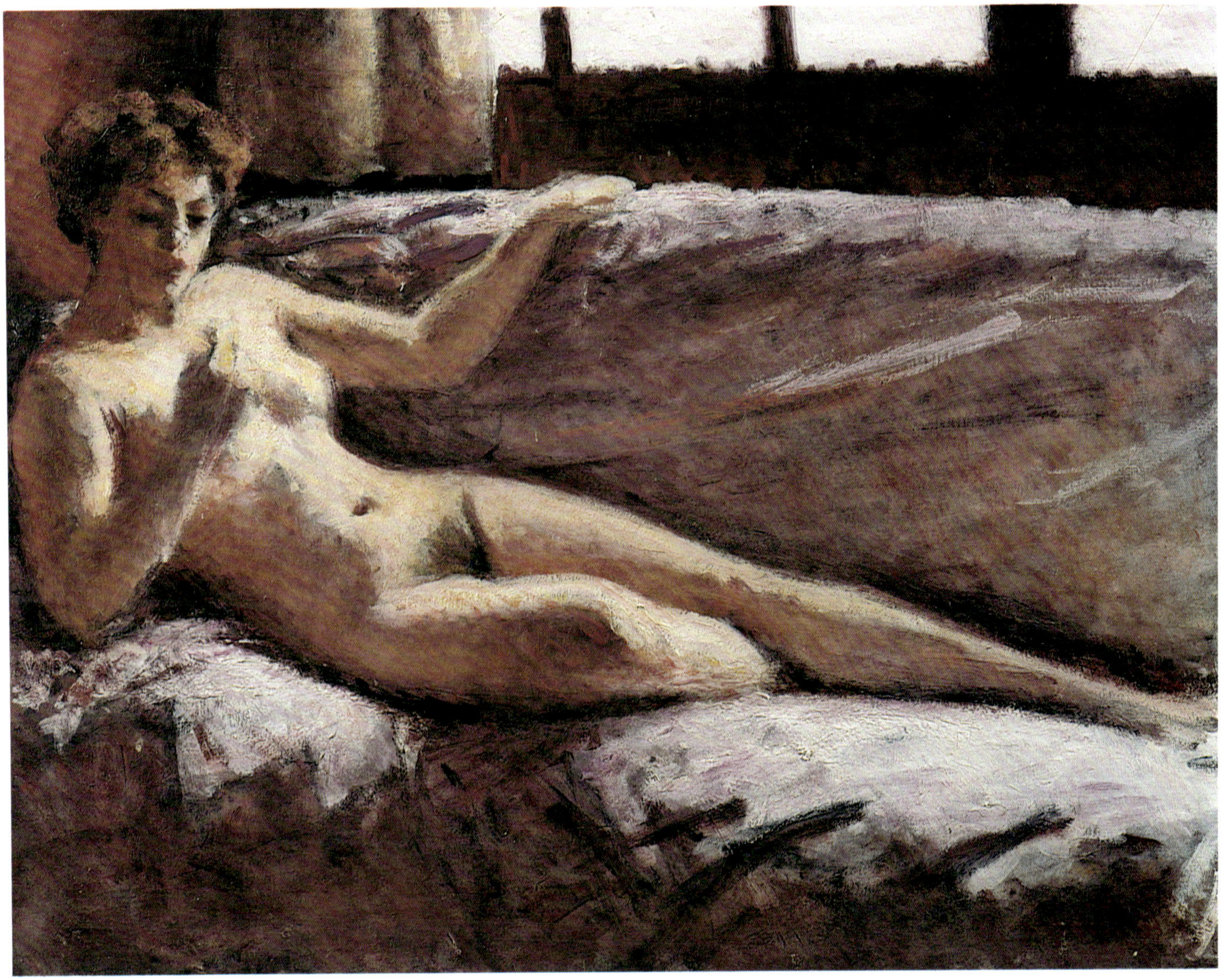

Oil on canvas
44.5 x 54.6 cms
s.t.l.f. O'Conor
d.t.l.f. '09
Insc: verso, on the stretcher bar, Nature Morte Roderic O'Conor No.5

Prov: M. Zeitline, Paris; private collection.

Exh: *Salon d'Automne* 1909 as (1321) Nature Morte

Private collection

Nature morte

Still life

This is a typical heavily painted 'nature morte' by O'Conor, deliberate in its composition and brilliantly illuminated with the light reflected from the white drapery on which the traditional objects of the still life have been placed.

We can identify these vessels (with the exception of the large pouring pot at the rear) as traditional domestic ware made in the local ceramics factory at Quimper in Brittany. O'Conor would probably have brought them back to Paris on his return to city life in 1904. Their frequent inclusion in Parisian studio pictures represents an emotional and nostalgic link to Brittany, and to the thirteen more or less continuous years which he had spent there.

The painting was probably exhibited in the 1909 Salon d'Automne as one of a group of six O'Conor pictures. In 1909 he was actually serving as Vice-President of the Salon along with Charles Plumet, with the Fauve painter Henri Manguin being exhibition organiser. O'Conor's election as Vice-President may be taken as an indication of the esteem within which he was held by his co-sociétaires at the Salon, although as we know from Bell he had no great liking for the job.[1]

This traditionally approached still life stands in marked contrast to O'Conor's earlier and more experimental work when he was in Brittany. Forms are carefully modelled, light is controlled for maximum effect, and although there is an impressive display of painterly control, there is nothing here that can be said to be experimental or adventurous when compared to some of the developments which were then taking place in French painting.

This picture, for example, was made and exhibited within four years of the emergence of the Fauve painters at the 1905 Salon, and a year after Braque's first cubist works. Picasso had painted his epic "Demoiselles d'Avignon" just two years earlier and Matisse's retrospective in the previous year at the 1908 Salon d'Automne had established him as a major talent. Yet O'Conor shows no sign in this painting of any inclination towards these new developments, preferring to keep to a style of painting which might best be described as expressive realism.

1. O'Conor in a letter to Clive Bell wrote that he found his duty on the jury to be 'a nasty job and a tiresome one'.The letter is undated but was written in 1909 after the Salon d'Automne had opened in October. Collection of the National Gallery of Ireland, Dublin. Among the artists whose work O'Conor would have reviewed and who were included in the exhibition were Brancusi, van Dongen, Duchamp, Matisse, Kandinsky, Gerald Kelly, John Lavery, Manguin, Maufra, Sickert, Villon and Vlaminck.

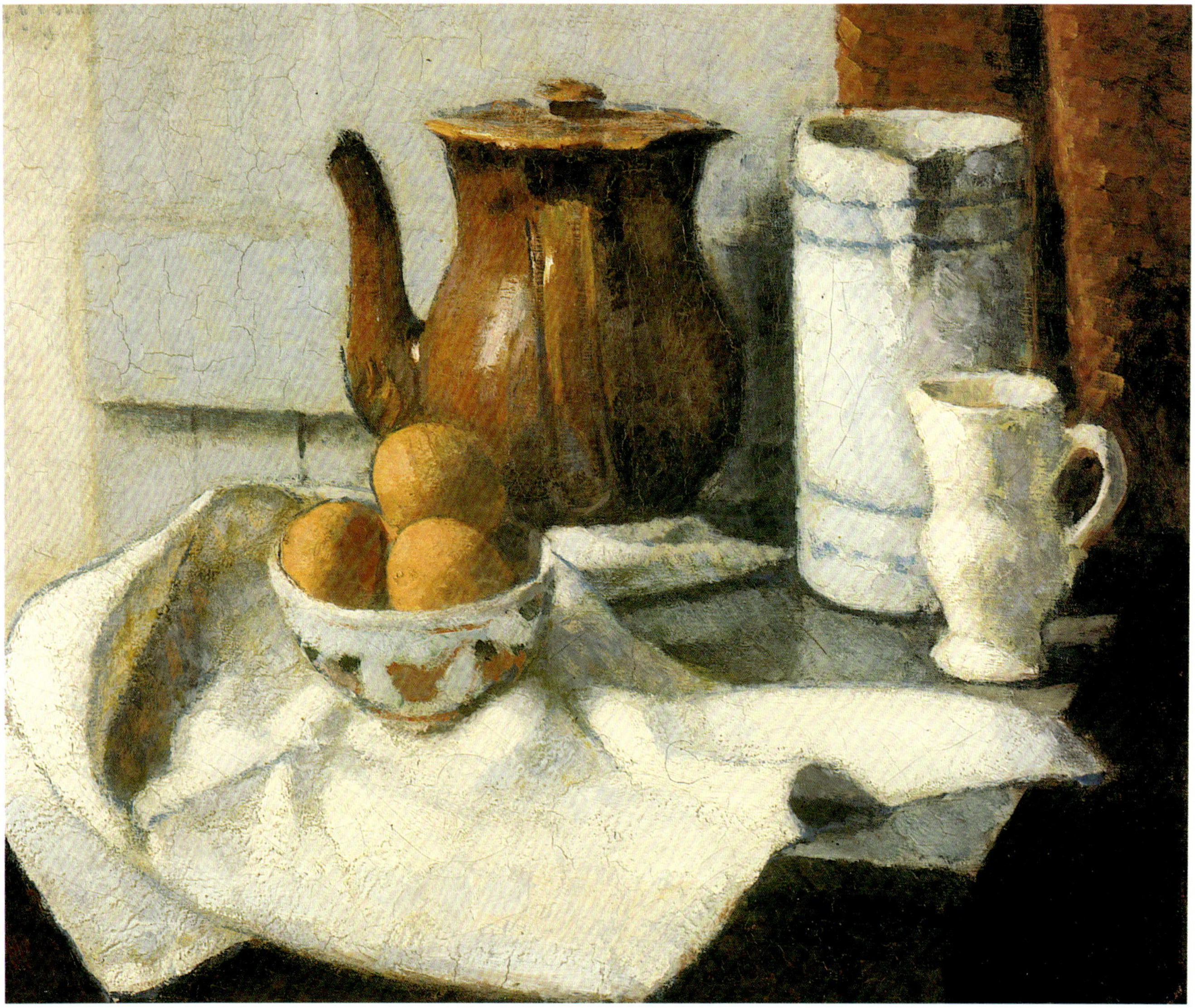

circa. 1914
Oil on canvas
46.3 x 65.6 cms.
Atelier stamp verso

Prov: Hôtel Drouot, Paris, Vente O'Conor, 1956; Browse and Darby, London 1982; Sotheby's, London, 2 November 1983, (68); Crane Kalman Gallery, London; J.G. Cooney; Pym's Gallery, London, 1986; private collection.

Exh: London, *Irish Renascence; Irish art in a century of change,* Pym's Gallery, 1986 (7) ill.

Lit: Benington 1992 (191)

Private collection

Bowl of roses

When O'Conor was in his rather drab studio in Montparnasse he often chose to paint flowers and bouquets to keep in touch with nature and the rich colour contrasts which he preferred in his landscapes. This particular example is composed on the diagonal, with the centrally placed flowers offset by the foreground bowl which echoes their colour in the bottom right hand corner. A slightly schematic curtain balances the composition through its entry into the picture in the top left. This arrangement suggests that O'Conor was trying to infuse this otherwise quite ordinary subject with some sense of implied visual movement between the three main compositional elements.

The use of a light reflecting surface gives a rich illumination to the leaves and flowers which have been deliberately chosen for their red and green complimentary colour contrast which he liked so much. As is usual with O'Conor there is the use of a lively paint surface which has been worked wet in wet in bold colour.

At the time of his death in 1940, O'Conor owned a number of Odilon Redon's prints, which he may have begun to collect as early as 1897.[1] Redon's work by 1900 had become a celebration of explosive colour and his flower pictures and pastels probably had some influence on O'Conor.

1. O'Conor's printmaking friend Armand Seguin sent him Redon's address and in the same letter passed on advice from Sérusier that if he was buying prints he could probably get a better price by buying directly from the artist. Seguin to O'Conor, letter No. 20, 23 June 1897. Sutton, Puget, Boyle-Turner eds.,*Une vie de Bohème*, Lausanne, 1989.

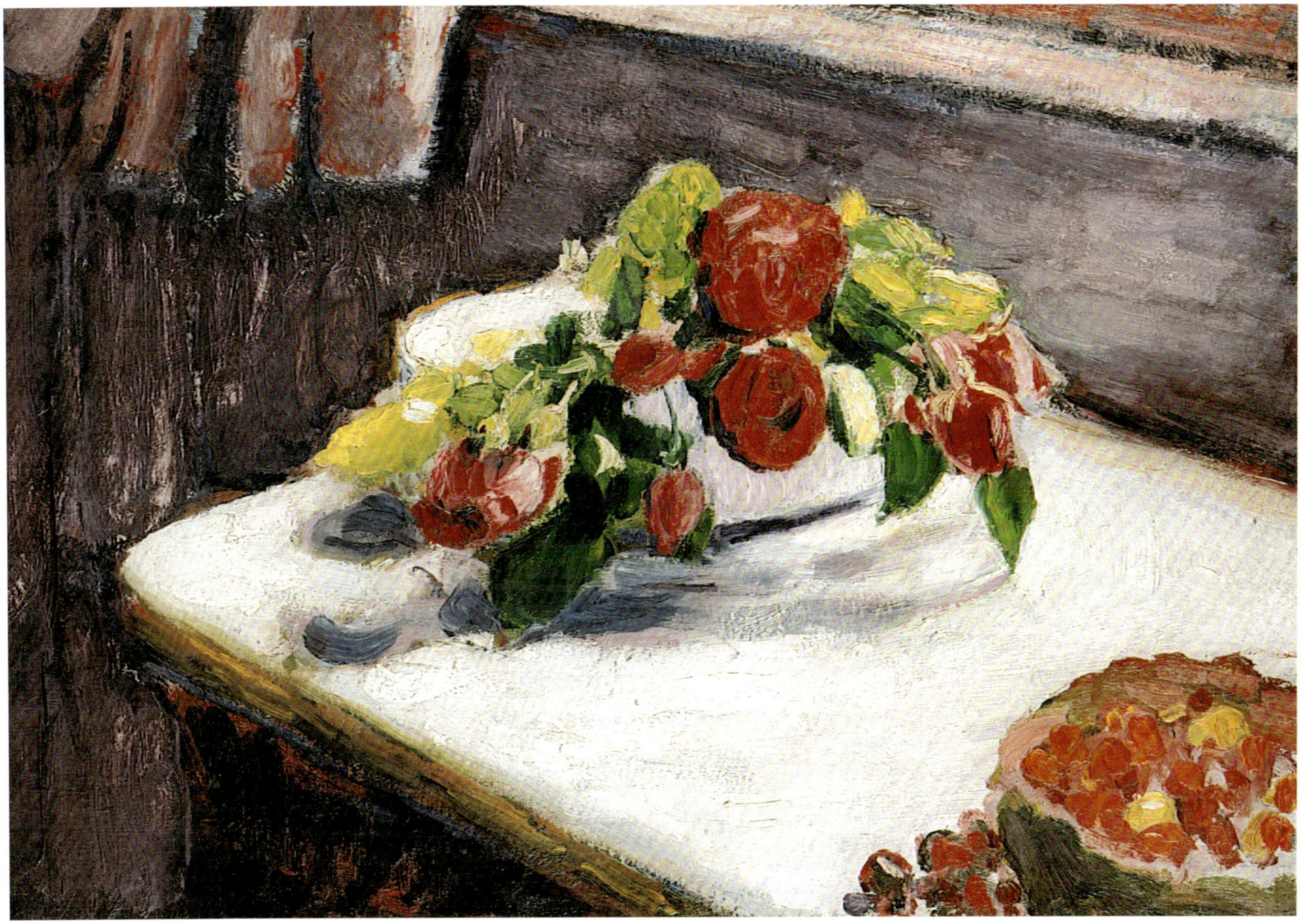

Oil on canvas
92.4 x 73.2 cms
s.b.l.f. O'Conor
d.b.l.f '15
Insc: verso, Fruits R. O'Conor.

Prov: Schoneman Gallery, New York; private collection U.S.A. 1960; private collection.

Exh: [?] Paris, *Salon d'Automne,* 1919 'Fruits'(1419).

Private collection

Nature morte - Fruits

Still life - Fruit

This still life may have been exhibited by O'Conor in 1919 as one of a group of nine paintings which he showed in the first Salon d'Automne exhibition to be held after the end of the 1914-1918 war. His paintings that year included one entitled 'Fruits' (1419) and this title appears on the stretcher bar of this particular work.

When he was working in his Paris studio, O'Conor liked to place his 'nature mortes' close to the large window which dominated one wall, and then set up his easel in the darker interior. From such a position the still life could be observed against the light. As a result the objects and forms become brightly illuminated by the natural light streaming into the studio, recalling the nineteenth century Impressionist tradition of painting 'contre-jour'. The brilliance of light and colour which O'Conor achieved through this means was probably in compensation for his not always having easy access to landscape motifs.

In this composition the objects of the still life have been placed close to the centre of a painting in which the background has been rather predictably divided into thirds using the verticals made by the wall, the curtains, and the window of the studio. Heavily painted and having a deliberately worked surface, it is likely that this picture was given this degree of attention and resolution for the Salon exhibition.

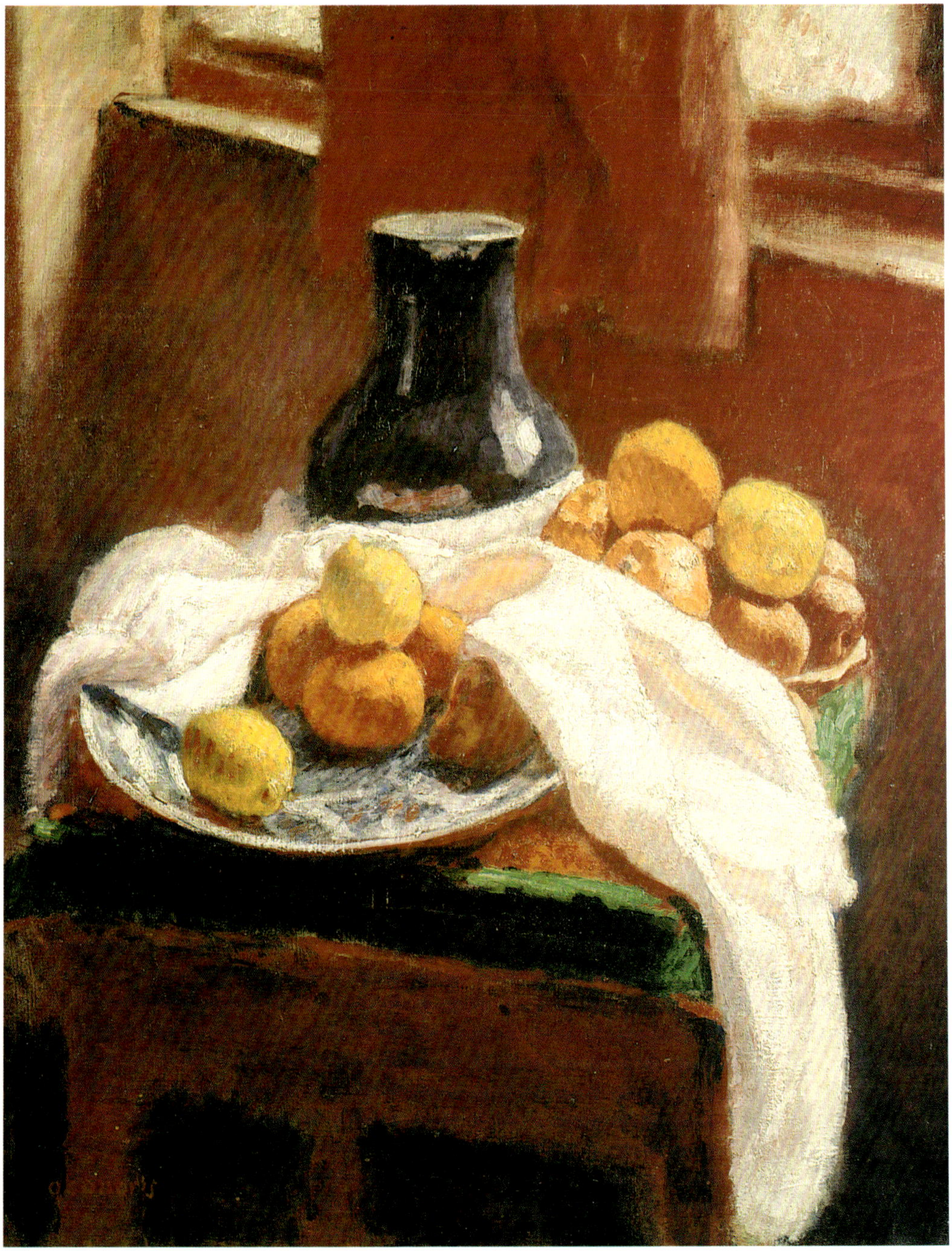

circa 1920
Oil on canvas
91.4 x 72.4 cms
Signed verso, on the stretcher bar Roderic O'Conor
Insc: verso, on the stretcher bar Roderic O'Conor 102 rue du Cherche Midi La Jeune Fille.

Prov: Purchased in Paris by present owner.

Exh: [?] *Salon d'Automne* 1928 (1508).

Lit: Benington (216) p.124.

Private collection

La jeune fille

The young girl

Although not positively identified, there is a similarity between this girl's appearance and that of O'Conor's model Renée Honta, the woman who became his mistress and who eventually married him in 1933 when he was 73 years of age and she was 39. Renée was born in Pau in 1894 but it is not known when she arrived in Paris or when she first met O'Conor.

If we could be certain that this is indeed Renée Honta, then we would have to conclude from her youthful appearance in this painting that she was quite young when O'Conor began to use her as his model. The earliest surviving record of a relationship between them comes from a letter which O'Conor wrote to Renée in 1916, (she would then have been twenty-two) and it is fairly evident from its contents that they were at that time already on intimate terms.

O'Conor has placed his model in a rather formal pose which acknowledges the classical tradition, with the light source from the studio window brilliantly illuminating the surface form. Although thickly painted with extensive use of the palette knife, the nude figure of this young woman is delicately and sensitively rendered. The manipulation of light across the body forms and the translucent quality of the skin tones are very convincing, given the palette knife technique which predominates.

The inscription on the stretcher bar gives rise to speculation that this may have been the picture which O'Conor exhibited in the 1928 Salon d'Automne. However if anything this only adds further uncertainty to the true identity of the sitter for if it is a painting of a youthful Renée, it is somewhat unlikely that there would have been such a long interval between the actual painting of this work and its eventual appearance in this exhibition.

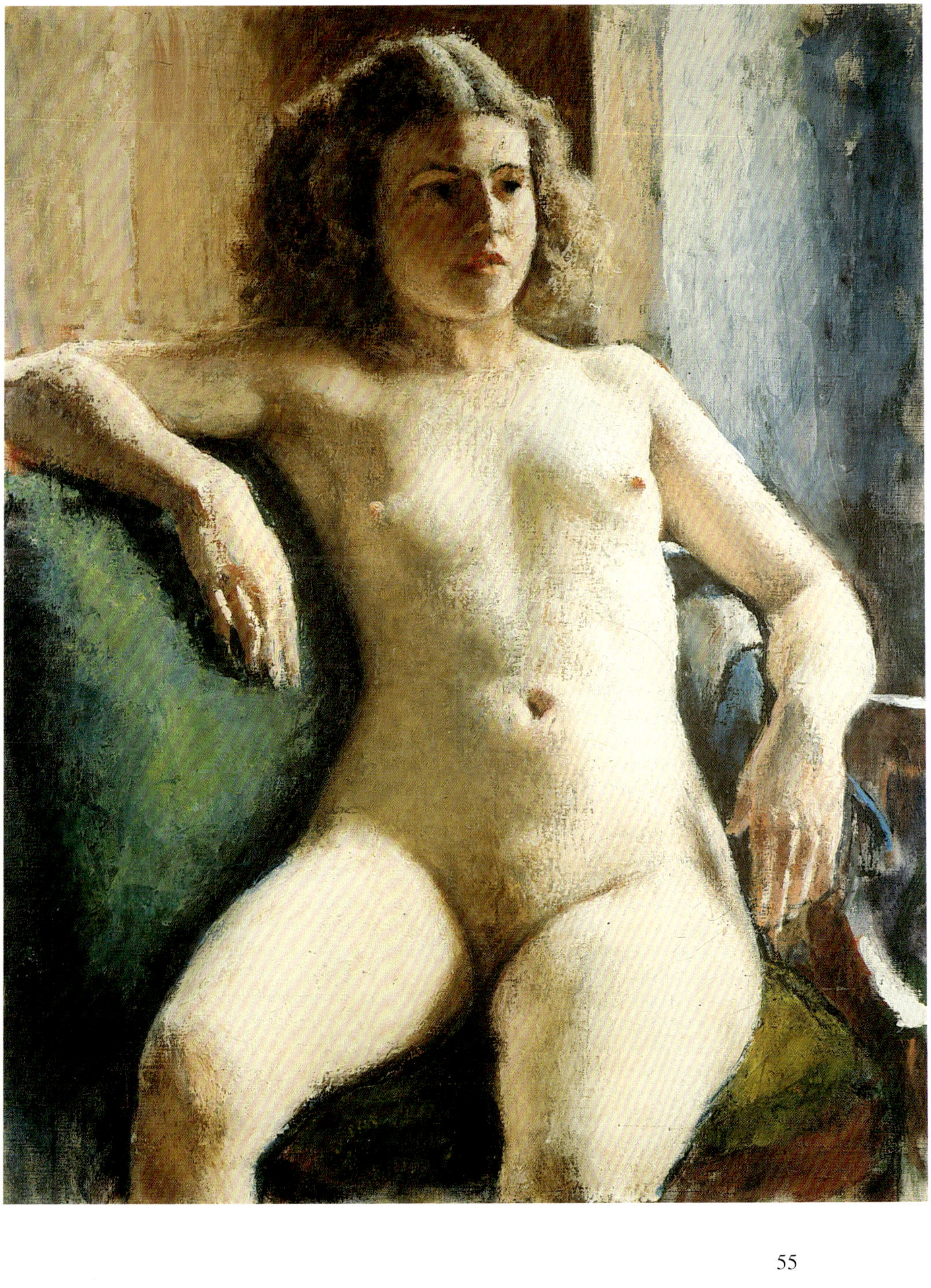

Bibliography

Publications on Roderic O'Conor

Sutton, Denys 'Roderic O'Conor, little known member of the Pont-Aven Circle', *Studio*, No.811, November 1960. pp.168-74 and 194-96

Lynch, Bryan 'Roderic O'Conor (1860-1940)' *ERA 5*, The Goldsmith Press Ltd, Co. Kildare, pp.19-23, 1980

O'Brian, John 'Morrice - O'Conor, Gauguin, Bonnard et Vuillard', *Revue de l'Universitè de Moncton,* vol. 15, nos. 2-3, 1982, pp. 9-34

Johnston, Roy 'Roderic O'Conor in Brittany', *Irish Arts Review,* Vol.1 No. 1, Spring 1984

Johnston, Roy *'Roderic O'Conor (1860-1940)'* Retrospective exhibition, Musée de Pont-Aven, France. 1984

Johnston, Roy 'Gauguin's Irish friend', *Art and Artists,* September 1984, pp.26-28

Benington, Jonathan 'From realism to expressionism: the early career of Roderic O'Conor', *Apollo,* April, 1985, pp.253-61

Wynne, Michael 'Two Roderic O'Conor drawings in Stockholm', *Burlington Magazine,* May 1985, pp. 302,304

Johnston, Roy *'Roderic O'Conor (1860-1940)'* Retrospective exhibition, Ulster Museum, Belfast and Barbican Art Gallery, London; National Gallery of Ireland Dublin; Whitworth Art Gallery, Manchester, 1985

Johnston, Roy 'Roderic O'Conor - the elusive personality', *Irish Arts Review,* Vol.2 No.4, Winter 1985 pp.31-40

Johnston, Roy 'O'Conor Gravures' in 'Pont-Aven et ses peintres à propos d'un centenaire', *Arts de L'Ouest,* Université de Rennes, 1986, pp. 139-54

Sutton, D., Puget C., Boyle-Turner C. eds. *Une Vie de Bohème,* lettres du peintre Armand Seguin à Roderic O'Conor, Lausanne, 1989

Johnston, Roy *'Roderic O'Conor (1860-1940)'* Ph.D. thesis, University of Dublin, Trinity College, 1992 (Unpublished)

Benington, Jonathan *Roderic O'Conor,* a biography with a catalogue of his work, Irish Academic Press, Blackrock 1992

Murphy, Paula *'Roderic O'Conor'* Town House in association with The National Gallery of Ireland, Dublin, 1992

Johnston, Roy 'O'Conor, Roderic Anthony, Irish painter', *The Dictionary of Art,* Macmillan, London, 1996

Chronology

1860 Roderic Anthony O'Conor born 17 October at Milton Co Roscommon.

1865 The O'Conors moved to Dublin and resided at 23 Waltham Terrace, Blackrock, living in subsequent years at 17 Sandymount Road (1867-69); 79 Wellington Road (1869-72); 9 Morehampton Road (1872-77); 88 Pembroke Road (1877-83); and 25 Pembroke Road (1883-93)

1873-78 Attended Ampleforth College in Yorkshire

1879-81 Attended the Metropolitan School of Art Dublin

1881-82 Attended Royal Hibernian Academy of Art, Dublin

1882-83 Attended Metropolitan School of Art, Dublin

1883-84 Attended Académie Royale des Beaux-Arts, d'Anvers

1884 Awarded the Taylor Prize at the Royal Dublin Society

1885 Exhibited at the Annual Royal Hibernian Academy Exhibition

1885-86 Attended the RHA for free study

1886-87? Studied with Carolus Duran in Paris. (?) Visited Pont-Aven, stayed at the Pension Gloanec and met J.Milner-Kite whom he knew from Antwerp.

1888 Exhibited at the Paris Salon

1889 Exhibited at the Paris Salon and the Salon des Indépendants

1890 Exhibited at the Salon des Indépendants

1891 Met Cuno Amiet in Paris, also Armand Seguin. Travelled to London and exhibited at the New English Art Club. Painted in Brittany at Pont Aven.

1892 In Pont-Aven early in the year, exhibited at the Salon des Indépendants. Visited Paris in spring and returned to Pont Aven on May 1 to stay at Pension Gloanec.

1893 Left Pont-Aven early in March to visit Filiger and Seguin at Le Pouldu. Worked throughout the summer with Seguin on a series of etchings. Painted with Amiet. His father Roderic Joseph O'Conor J.P. High Sheriff of County Roscommon, died on October 14 and the artist returned to Ireland for some months.

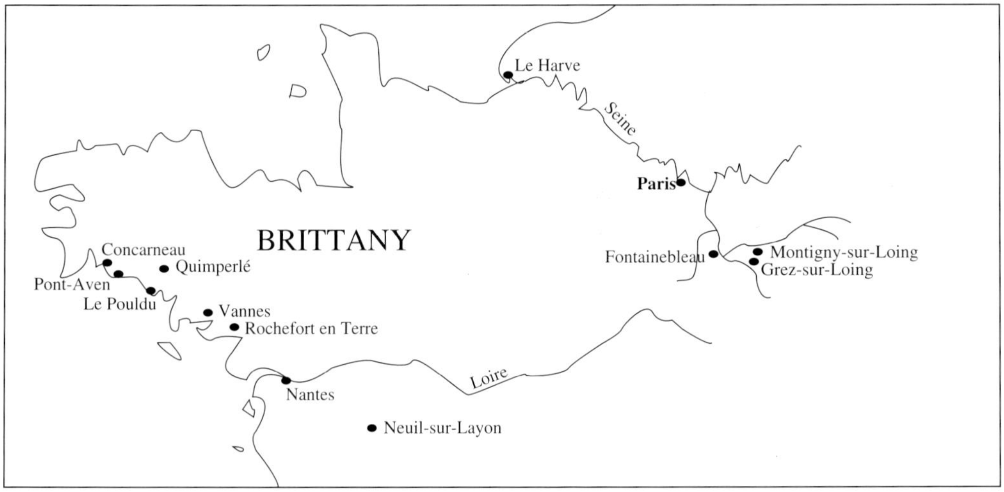

Sketch map of northern France

1894 Returned to Pont Aven in the spring. Exhibited at the Barc de Boutteville's Gallery in the 6th exhibition of Impressionist and Symbolist painters in March, 7th exhibition in July, 8th exhibition in November. Developed a close friendship with Paul Gauguin in Pont-Aven. On 25 May visited Concarneau with Gauguin, Anna the Javanese, Seguin, Jourdan and female companions. Received from Gauguin the gift of a monoprint - *The Angelus in Brittany* - dedicated; "for my friend O'Conor, one man of Samoa, P.Gauguin 1894". In December the artist went to Grez-sur-Loing.

1895 Bought the painting *Te Nave Nave Fenua* by Gauguin. O'Conor went to Grez-sur-Loing in March. Exhibited at the Barc-de-Boutteville's 10th exhibition in September. Went to Rochefort-en-Terre, Morbihan, in December.

1896/7 At Rochefort-en-Terre.

1898 Invited to exhibit with "La Libre Esthétique" in Brussels with Denis, Ensor, Maillol, Ranson, Van Rysselberghe and others.

1899-1902 At Pont-Aven

1903 Began to exhibit annually at the Salon des Indépendants and annually thereafter until 1908. Exhibited with Bonnard, Gauguin, Marquet, Matisse, Moret, Rouault, Vallotton, Vuillard and others in the inaugural exhibition of the Salon D'Automne, and annually thereafter until 1935 with the exception of 1907, 1914-18 and 1933.

1904 At Pont-Aven and visited Filiger at Le Pouldu. Moved from Brittany to live at 102 rue du Cherche-Midi, Paris. Met Clive Bell. Exhibited *Une Jeune Bretonne* at Guildhall Art Gallery in London, in an exhibition of works by Irish painters organised by Hugh Lane.

1905 Second invitation to exhibit with "La Libre Esthétique" in Brussels. Bought Cezanne's lithograph, *Les Baigneuses* from the Parisien dealer Vollard. The Russian collector Ivan Morozov purchased his painting, *Repos* from the Salon des Indépendants exhibition, now in the collection of the Hermitage Museum St Petersburg.

1906 Corresponded with Maurice Denis.

1907 Served on the jury for the Salon d'Automne, the exhibition included Sickert, Rouault, Redon, Modigliani, Matisse, Derain, Dufy, Braque and Bonnard.

1908 Exhibited at the Allied Artists Association, Albert Hall London in July.

1909 Elected joint Vice-President with Charles Plumet of the Salon d'Automne jury.

1910 Visited Italy.

1912 Visited Spain.

1913 Rented Villa Marguerite, in Cassis, Bouches de Rhone and painted there in the summer. In Paris for the Salon d'Automne, returned to Cassis until the end of the year.

1919 Met Matthew Smith in Paris. Invited by Clive Bell to meet Derain.

1920 Frequent contact with Roger Fry in Paris.

1923 Exhibited at the Salon des Tuileries, then annually until 1928 and again in 1930

1933 Married Renée Honta in Paris on 24 October. They lived at Neuil-sur-Layon.

1934 At Torremolinos in Spain.

1935 At Torremolinos then in Paris and at Neuil-sur-Layon.

1940 Roderic O'Conor died in his home at Neuil-sur-Layon on 18 March.

1955 Madame O'Conor died in Paris on 22 January.

1956 Dispersal sale of studio contents of Roderic O'Conor and Renée Honta at Hôtel Drouot Paris on 6/7 February.